THE EMPIRE STATE BUILDING—1931
SHREVE, LAMB & HARMON, *Architects*

ASPECTS OF THE SOCIAL HISTORY OF AMERICA

BY

THEODORE SIZER
ANDREW C. McLAUGHLIN
DIXON RYAN FOX
HENRY SEIDEL CANBY

CHAPEL HILL
THE UNIVERSITY OF NORTH CAROLINA PRESS
1931

COMPOSED AND PRINTED IN THE UNITED STATES OF AMERICA BY EDWARDS
AND BROUGHTON COMPANY, AND BOUND BY L. H. JENKINS, INC.

MARY TUTTLE BOURDON LECTURES
MOUNT HOLYOKE COLLEGE

1930-1931

The University of North Carolina Press, Chapel Hill, N. C.; The Baker and Taylor Company, New York; Oxford University Press, London; Maruzen-Kabushiki-Kaisha, Tokyo; Edward Evans & Sons, Ltd., Shanghai; D. B. Centen's Wetenschappelijke Boekhandel, Amsterdam.

TABLE OF CONTENTS

THE MARY TUTTLE BOURDON LECTURES AT MOUNT HOLYOKE COLLEGE

FOREWORD

THE FOUR lectures gathered in this book show various aspects of the development experienced by Massachusetts and other eastern sections of the American Commonwealth during their first three hundred years. Given at Mount Holyoke College on a foundation established by the Alumnae Association in honor of a woman, they illustrate in that very fact the stride of time.

A community has always the problem in celebrating its history of doing justice both to its founders and to itself, of so understanding its past as to understand to some good purpose its own present. The New England of our day suffers from diverse estimates, according to the view of its Puritan inheritance which is chosen by one or another critic. We have learned to distrust anything like Fourth of July oratory. But in commemorating the tercentenary of the Massachusetts Bay Colony many New Englanders have gained something better than a complacent sense of past glories.

The lectures here presented interpret American ideas with the advantage of perspectives given by time and by modern scholarship. On a basis of facts sometimes neglected but in general familiar, they show the significance of performances which have suffered too often from false evaluations. They clarify, in more than one respect, our view of the past.

LIST OF ILLUSTRATIONS

THE DEVELOPMENT OF
AMERICAN ART

THE DEVELOPMENT OF AMERICAN ART

BY THEODORE SIZER

As we are celebrating this year the three hundredth anniversary of the founding of this Commonwealth, let us consider, briefly and dispassionately, the extent of our artistic contributions. Much can happen in three centuries, a period corresponding, for instance, to that extending from the rude beginnings of Greek civilization to the death of Alexander the Great and from the earliest efforts of Giotto to the latest of Tintoretto. In other words, it is a length of time corresponding to the birth and maturity of the two greatest artistic epochs. We may, in defense, protest at the seeming unfairness of such a comparison and argue that, after all, our greatest efforts were expended and lavished in every field of endeavor other than art and literature. Nevertheless, we cannot escape from the unpleasant fact that the fullest expression of any civilization is to be found in its cultural, rather than in its political or industrial achievements. We are not particularly interested today in the business enterprises of the Venetians, the branch banking of the Medici, or the political boundaries of ancient Greece. Greek business men are forgotten, except in so far as their names have been preserved by sculptors on the most beautiful of grave-steles.

3

If we stop to think of it, the history of American taste, like that of Greece, is written in our cemeteries. The earliest settlers left their graves unmarked lest their reduced numbers be noted by over-curious Indians. Our Colonial tombstones are simple, direct, unaffected, and dignified. Well-proportioned and spaced letters are sometimes surmounted by little frowning, forbidding looking cupids or by weeping willow trees. Occasionally one meets a more elaborate table-tomb reminiscent of peaceful English parish graveyards. Fitness, sincerity, and just proportion are the rule. Fenollosa once wrote that "all art is harmonious spacing under special technical conditions that vary." This applies equally well to much Colonial lettering, to the Parthenon, or to the typography of Bruce Rogers. A decade or two before and after the Civil War such fundamentals were forgotten. The aesthetic taste and discrimination of the western world seem to have collapsed under the baneful influence of Romanticism and the uncontrolled and misunderstood forces of Industrialism. The cemetery of this epoch is without dignity, charm, or restraint. Mawkish angels with upturned eyes, broken columns, draped urns, bad lettering, polished granite, and cast-iron benches are the order of the day. Fortunately our native reticence saved us from the theatricality and unpleasant realism of the over sentimental sculpture in the cemeteries of many Latin countries.

4

DEVELOPMENT OF ART

All but a few of our Civil War memorials are a monotonous series of granite or cast-iron soldiers, displaying the most extraordinary family resemblance, conveniently clad in winter overcoats, and perpetually standing at "parade rest." In a certain town in northern Ohio, famed for sewer pipe production, one of these dismal effigies of a volunteer has been actually placed in a fountain where its clothes have been kept continuously wet for the past half century or more. The South, being too poor to afford such machine-made tributes, alone was spared. If it will make us feel any better, the new Guards Monument behind Whitehall in London, though it would delight the exacting eye of any drill sergeant, is lifeless, uninspired, and dull. The cemeteries of the nineties succumbed to the correct and imitative classicism of McKim, Meade, and White; little pagan temples superseding the rusticated Romanesque of the previous age. The memorials to our civil and military dead are, in our own time, a great and significant step, far in advance of anything we have previously done during our one hundred and fifty-four years of Independence. The whole world has progressed mightily in such things. Manship's memorial of J. P. Morgan in the Metropolitan, Gill's superb lettering at New College, Oxford, and the Great War memorial in Munich all point to a new and better day.

Let us, however, concern ourselves with the art of the living. Foreign visitors to our shore are often disappointed not to find the imagined pioneer qualities of American civilization more apparent in our art. The original settlers of the Atlantic seaboard were not of the romantic pioneer type popularized in Europe by Hollywood. The covered wagon, moreover, came two centuries after the settlement of Massachusetts Bay. Communities first came as homogeneous and compact units and established themselves and shaped their surroundings as nearly in accordance with their previous environment as was possible. This is equally true of the Puritans of New England, the Dutch of New York, the Swedes of Delaware, the Germans in Pennsylvania, and the English squires of Virginia. Scattered immigration came much later. These people adapted themselves to the society of the earlier settlers. The same conditions were perpetuated in the successive waves of emigration and settlement west of the Allegheny Mountains. The further our ancestors got from their European source the more tenaciously they clung to their traditions. We are transplanted Europeans, not a new race, as is sometimes believed of us, and our art from the very beginning down to the time of the Great War has been provincial European.

Spain, we often forget, explored, conquered, and settled large sections of this hemisphere, a century

PLATE I

Courtesy of the Gallery of Fine Arts, Yale University

GENERAL WASHINGTON AT THE BATTLE OF TRENTON
BY JOHN TRUMBULL (1756-1843)

before our English forebears. The great Cathedral in Mexico City was begun in 1573, one hundred and fifty-nine years before Independence Hall in Philadelphia, our finest and most monumental pre-Revolutionary public building. The seventeenth- and eighteenth-century churches and Jesuit missions in New Mexico and Texas, admixtures of Spanish baroque and the native pueblo, did not, however, have any perceptible influence on our architectural style until the recent influx of coupon-clipping Easterners to southern California. Our ancestors knew nothing of the splendors of contemporary Spanish architecture.

They, rather plain townspeople, artisans, and indentured servants, came to these shores for a variety of reasons, economic pressure and desire for religious freedom being the chief among them. That the Pilgrims were townsfolk is well illustrated by the fact that they nearly starved to death during their first year in a country abounding with game and were only rescued by a shipment of supplies from England, which manifestation of Providence we annually celebrate with roast turkey and cranberry sauce. These transplanted city dwellers lost no time in recreating in the wilderness European conditions as far as it was possible. There was not the slightest attempt to establish new customs, manners, religion, and, least of all, art. The original Massachusetts architecture was in the form of

7

conical huts of branches, rushes, and turf, resembling the hovels of neolithic man. The origin of these crude shelters is to be found in the charcoal burners' and shepherds' huts of England. The transition from these temporary habitations and from the analogous log cabins of the Swedes in Delaware was rapid. Their early frame houses show many interesting survivals of the Gothic—steep roofs, casement windows, clustered chimneys, quaint irregularities, open construction, and functional honesty. St. Luke's Church near Smithfield, Virginia, the earliest brick church now standing in America, with its high pitched roof, great square tower, buttresses, and pointed arched windows with tracery is Gothic, showing only a hint or two of the coming change in taste. Brick houses, such as the Jacobean Bacon's Castle, built before 1676, were rare in America, although common in contemporary England. There during the seventeenth century, masonry largely supplanted wood, due to the scarcity of oak caused by the building of naval and trading vessels and to the constant fear of fire engendered by the great conflagration in London in 1666. In America the vast majority of houses were of frame. Towns were far from crowded. Forests had to be cleared, wood was cheap, and building lime scarce. We are all familiar with such examples of wooden Gothic as the "House of Seven Gables." The type of dwelling varies as we travel down the coast, individual

8

development being due more to inherited tradition than to local environment.

These differences were more marked in the next century as the colonists grew in wealth and became more concerned with their surroundings. Our great pre-Revolutionary development coincides with the change in England from the style of the Middle Ages to that of the Renaissance. Inigo Jones and Sir Christopher Wren worked "after the good Roman manner" and did not "follow the Gothic Rudeness of the Old Design," to quote the diarist Evelyn. In spite of the happy introduction of the Georgian style, earlier traditions lingered. To give but two of a dozen familiar examples, General Lee's family home, "Stratford," built just a century after the death of King James, and "Tuckahoe" near Richmond, which dates from a few years later, are, nevertheless, Jacobean in plan. Jacobean motives survived in our household furniture long after they had ceased to be used in our mother country. We have been traditionalists from the beginning.

The great manors on the James River, those in Philadelphia, Boston, Salem, Portsmouth, and elsewhere, built after 1700, follow the new Renaissance style of England with an exactitude that is surprising. One has only to compare, not only plans and elevations but details of fireplaces, mouldings, and panelling to the engraved designs in the score or more of English architectural publications to appreciate how utterly dependent our "Colonial style" is on the Georgian. The published sources of our information were of the best and our forefathers, perhaps because they had no other, used them. The eighteenth century was an age when the educated gentleman felt it necessary to know something of architecture. Our master carpenters and builders knew their Vitruvius, Palladio, Jones, Wren, and Gibbs. Instead of Lord Burlington, William Kent, Batty Langley, Asher Benjamin, and other such excellent sources of material, the present-day builder and his client are more familiar with the advertisements in the *Saturday Evening Post* and possibly the *House Beautiful*. Diffusion of the good, the bad, and the indifferent has superseded the earlier limitation to the best. It is only recently that we have built Italian villas in Maine and the Gothic of northern France in the swamps of Florida. Formerly there were no architects, schools, or art critics—nothing but a great tradition.

English forms were often simplified. The heaviness and pomposity of the Georgian was thus avoided. This elimination of elaboration can best be appreciated in comparing contemporary English silver with the best efforts of our Colonial craftsmen. We have never surpassed the purity of form, dignity, and functional design of such pieces as may be seen in the Mabel Brady Garvan Collection at

PLATE II

Courtesy of the Gallery of Fine Arts, Yale University

COFFEE POT
BY JACOB HURD OF BOSTON (1702-1758)

Yale. Simplicity and vigor of design were had, but the ruggedness of "pioneer art" is absent.

The same is true of our early painters; they too were provincials, not pioneers. Their first and chief concern was portraiture, which like architecture and what we now term the decorative arts, was not considered "art." The Puritan had the deep-rooted conviction that all art was essentially immoral, the lingering traces of which still curse us. He failed to see that art does, after all, satisfy a fundamental human instinct. We cannot be without it. But houses were small and presented little wall space suitable for decoration. The nonconformity of our churches precluded both sculpture and painting. The few feeble portraitists of the end of the seventeenth and the first quarter of the eighteenth centuries, who either visited or settled in the Colonies were "face painters" of the tavern sign and coach tradition. John Smibert, who came to this country in 1729, got his start in the ancient craft of coach painting (a profession which preserved many early Italian Renaissance technical methods long after they had been forgotten by artists). It was Smibert who first introduced the main current of European painting. He was a fellow pupil of Hogarth's at the London Academy of Sir James Thornhill. One can observe many characteristics of the younger and vastly more talented satirists in the "Bishop Berkeley and His Family" at Yale. The native, John Singleton

Copley, stepson of one of the earliest American engravers, Peter Pelham, was trained in Europe. Through Benjamin West and his many gifted pupils, such as Gilbert Stuart, Charles Wilson Peale, and John Trumbull, the great tradition of English eighteenth-century portraiture—that of Reynolds, Romney, Gainsborough, and Raeburn—was planted on our shores. The efforts of this group, however, fall as far short of those of the principal Royal Academicians, as the latters' efforts do of those of Raphael, Giorgione, and Titian. The often naïve and fumbling, though always sincere, productions of both our Colonial master builders and painters were the fruit of an ancient and unbroken European tradition—traditions which were lost even to Europe in the holocaust of the French Revolution.

Until about that time there had been an orderly progression of styles, each growing gradually and logically out of its predecessor. The last of these, the rococo, typified, like the Gothic, the restless spirit of the North. This style, however, was associated with Monarchy. During the second half of the eighteenth century a series of interesting political, social, and archaeological events turned men's minds again to the grandeur that was Rome's. Statesmen and soldiers alike in our Revolutionary War drew much of their inspiration from the ancient Republic, and, as many new buildings were necessary, it was quite natural that they should seek guidance from the recent available architectural and archaeological publications, which were more plentifu than generally supposed. As most of these sources were excellent the resulting classical impulse was pleasing. Architectural and decorative elements in stone were translated with great skill into terms of wood, and the dignity, repose, and strength of Classical forms preserved. In this impluse there was none more influential than Thomas Jefferson, the only architect to become President of the United States. Commissioned to build the Capitol at Richmond he drew his inspiration from the Maison Carrée at Nîmes, the most perfect Roman temple existent. Others were quick to follow his example. He retired to his remodelled Monticello, a commanding and dignified mansion, hardly in keeping with our modern conceptions of Jeffersonian simplicity. Napoleon gave official sanction to the rising forces of Classicism of the reign of Louis XVI. His conception of a proper background was that of Imperial and not Republican Rome. His temple of victory, now the Church of the Madeleine, was built twenty-two years after the Capitol at Richmond which, to our credit, antedates anything similar in Europe. There are many manifestations of the French "Empire style" in American architecture and furniture, modified again, however, to conform to a simpler environment.

A second Classical impetus took place after the Greek War of Independence, in 1820, both Europe and America becoming conscious, for the first time, of the superiority of Greek architecture and sculpture. Greek forms followed Roman; banks, churches, college and government buildings, and private houses were all made in unquestioned imitation of pagan temples. These temples in antiquity had offered an adequate solution for a ritual that took place in a sunny climate out of doors. No one seems to have questioned, however, the use of the Greek portico in our northern latitudes, where it needlessly darkens interiors. The name of Nicholas Biddle of Philadelphia should be remembered as our chief Hellenist enthusiast, as Jefferson had been our Roman champion.

American sculpture had its tardy beginnings at the end of our Classical Revival over two hundred years after the founding of Massachusetts Bay Colony. Neo-classical insincerity and coldness are exemplified in the work of such men as Hiram Powers, William Rush, Horatio Greenough, and Ball Hughes. Unintelligent imitations of the antique persisted in coinage until it was reformed by the late President Roosevelt. Antiquarianism in any form is a fatal blow to style development.

A reaction set in against things classical about 1840 and brought with it the Romantic movement, which had had its architectural beginnings as far

PLATE III

Courtesy of the Gallery of Fine Arts, Yale University

AMERICAN COUNTRY LIFE: MAY MORNING (1855)
THE FOUR SEASONS OF LIFE: OLD AGE (1868)
CURRIER & IVES

back as 1753 with Walpole's Strawberry Hill. Post-offices, penitentiaries, railroad stations, academies, clubs, and private houses were all built in misconceived Gothic. As at Strawberry Hill, wood was substituted for stone forms, resulting in the gingerbread excrescences of "Carpenters' Gothic." Cast-iron was also used in the place of the more expensive stone clustered columns in many of our neo-mediaeval churches. Mouldings, filigree work, tracery, and other ornament could be had at wholesale from up-to-date iron foundries. Modern scholarship has made Gothic architecture archaeologically correct—and still-born. The supports of Brooklyn Bridge with their lancet openings are preferable to the authenticity of our modern churches, cathedrals, and college buildings.

Through the fifties down to the seventies Romanticism ran riot. Ruskin was read, the Waverley Novels were in everybody's hands, and to cap the climax the good Queen Victoria, or rather her unappreciated Consort, decided to hold a great exhibition. The Crystal Palace Exhibition of 1851 had its American counterpart in Philadelphia in 1876. Scarcely ever in the history of the world's art has taste been at such low ebb. The forces of the Industrial Revolution were misunderstood and misinterpreted. Studied picturesqueness was hopelessly entangled in machinery. It is only recently that we have ceased to be slaves of the machine and have mastered mass-production, though the Pullman Company still persists in spending vast sums on the clever but misguided application of wood grain on steel interiors. Other curious modern survivals of Victorianism are to be found, for instance, in the scroll work and job lithographer's lettering in our new small paper currency. The depths of our General Grant era were paralleled in the Queen's England and in the France of Louis Philippe.

The period just prior to and of the Civil War saw, however, the rise of our national school of landscape and figure painting, with which we associate such names as Cole, Durand, Bierstadt, and above all, Winslow Homer. Sentimentality and realism are both present in the sculptural groups of Rogers. We have already spoken of memorials turned out by the machine shop. The trend of American taste before and after the War between the States can be best observed from the wood-engraved illustrations in *Harper's Weekly* of the period. The badly drawn and colored, though intriguing, lithographs of Currier and Ives (termed "barber shop art" by the late Joseph Pennell) give us the same thing a few decades later. Our hopeless floundering like that of the rest of the world, was quite natural. The transition from the horse and carriage to the steam engine, from the sailing ship to the steamer, from mounted couriers to the telegraph, the rise of

16

Darwinism and the scientific awakening, the many powerful and conflicting forces, were duly reflected in the hybrid art of the period. Dreadful as it is, we must admit that much of it has decided character. We are indifferent to mediocrity and heed only excellence or down-right crudity.

A great awakening followed the excesses of Romanticism, culminating with the World's Fair of '93, the great turning point in American taste. For a generation previous our best architects had ceased to content themselves with published designs of current foreign styles, and went to Europe to study and gain first-hand knowledge. The result was an inspired, though not altogether happy, eclecticism. Public buildings were done in the Classical or in a strict Renaissance style. Banks continued to be Roman or Greek temples, and churches Mediaeval forgeries. In the hands of a master like Richardson, great possibilities were realized in the Romanesque. Palatial mansions were imitations of everything from Blois to Fontainebleau. Fantastic Gothic railroad stations gave way to huge edifices based on the Roman bath. The past became a vast grab bag. Miscellaneous and unrelated styles were drawn out at will and served up to meet any modern need. Factories, power stations, and machine shops were about the only types of buildings which were not stylized. Interiors reflected the same eclecticism. The Tudor, Florentine Renaissance, Georgian,

Louis XV, and a dozen other styles were, and still are, unfortunately, used indiscriminately. The impossibility of re-creation either of the spirit or the circumstances which gave rise to various types of architecture and decoration was lost sight of. The resulting jumble of imitations was manifestly insincere. Paradoxically, in our concern over "styles" we lost all "style." Great harm was done by popular travel and half digested learning. The wife of the returning millionaire wanted her house an imitation of a Francis I chateau—and architects must live! Fortunately we are now emerging from a second chaotic period of style-mongering.

Painters and sculptors down to the period of the Great War not only sought their education in Europe but, if possible, also lived there. This is true in painting from Whistler to Sargent, and in sculpture from Saint Gaudens to Manship. Each new movement in European art, be it Impressionism or Cubism, has had its counterpart in America. Although most of our students are now trained in this country we can scarcely be said to have yet made these two arts national in character. Sculpture is essentially a popular art and, as yet, the public is not sufficiently conscious of plastic form. In painting the emphasis is still on the easel pictures, painted in vast quantities for no one or for no place in particular. Our mural painting at the turn of the century was far from mediocre. We have, however,

Plate IV

Courtesy of the Addison Gallery of American Art, Phillips Academy

Eight Bells
by Winslow Homer (1836-1910)

recently abandoned the sterile symbols of Justice, Virtue, and Truth, though the beehive is still the favorite motive of the savings banks and sculptured owls clutter Yale's new buildings. The demand for murals should be greater. We have a number of excellent men. It is interesting to witness the rebirth of a national school of painting in Mexico since the Revolution of 1910. The great murals of Rivera and his colleagues have a vitality and local flavor about them which is entirely lacking with us.

The misinterpretation of half-understood scientific propositions is responsible for much bad work in paint on both sides of the Atlantic. Meaningless abstractions, wanting in design, have been one of the many evil results. But in this we are to blame; we get no better art than we deserve. A large section of the American public is either indifferent or actively hostile to the newer forms of expressions and damns them all. Our up-to-dateness stops with science, business methods, mechanics, and medicine. Our taste may be that of the seventies, but we may be sure that our bookkeeping methods and radio equipment are modern. It would never occur to any of us to have our surgeon use fine old Colonial technique, but we fill our house with imitation Colonial without a whimper. We accept the latest scientific discoveries without a thought but too often insist upon having the same old thing in art. Fortunately, or unfortunately, we cannot be Jacobean, French eighteenth century, or even American Colonial, nor should we wish to be. Until we cease apeing worn-out styles and live aesthetically, as well as mechanically and scientifically, in the twentieth century, our art will amount to as little as modern statesmanship does in backward-looking China. Our indifference to natural beauty is well illustrated by our toleration of the sign-board. The *Boston Transcript* recently published the following extraordinary information derived from North Carolina: "At forty miles an hour the tourist on the road from Durham to Raleigh passes a billboard every 6 seconds on the average. On the road from Beaufort to Asheville, 383 miles, he passes a billboard every 13 ½ seconds. The countless snipe signs (small posters on trees and fences), if included would more than double the figure. On Route 50, cross-state from Virginia to South Carolina, are 1,524 billboards, an average of one every 10 ½ seconds. The beautiful approaches to Asheville, 'land of the sky,' are smothered by huge flocks of billboards. And so it goes." Unpleasant facts such as these are, in part, offset by our really great art patronage. In 1929 we spent over two hundred and fifty millions for this purpose, something unparalleled in our history.

The architect has, however, an easier time than the artist. He practices a "practical" profession. But even in this there is a dark side to the picture.

DEVELOPMENT OF ART

The American Institute of Architects published a statement a short while ago, that during the year 1929, despite the falling off in building, "something over four billions of dollars in new structures were expended in cities and towns in this country. Yet it is estimated that three billion dollars worth of these structures were so ugly, so badly planned, so inappropriately located, or on such narrow or inconvenient streets as to have been a liability instead of an asset, almost from the day they were completed." The waste involved, as a natural result of man's inclination to destroy what is ugly in buildings, is described as "the greatest economic waste of our time."

The development of an American style has, nevertheless, definitely begun. We are no longer dependent on Europe for art instruction. We believe we have better here. It is the architects who are leading, and, in a lesser degree, our master printers, both professions being eminently utilitarian. We have almost ceased imitating Europe's past performances. Scientific discoveries and new materials, such as "Duco" and "Allegheny metal," are having extremely interesting and significant effects. The cultivated and inquisitive European is vastly more interested in our recent skyscrapers, our new methods of construction, and functional use of materials and ornament, than in our occasional sculpture and acres of paint. Our ability to attract great works of art across the ocean in the last analysis is a financial and not a creative one. We have, nevertheless, organized and housed our great art collections, as we have catalogued our libraries, far better than it has ever been done before. The tide is beginning to turn. It is Europe which is now looking to us for inspiration, as yet only in architecture, usually the forerunner in any artistic new movement. After three hundred years we have commenced to contribute something new, something distinctly American, to the art of the world. We never were "pioneers," but we have ceased to be "provincials."

SOME REFLECTIONS ON THE
AMERICAN REVOLUTION

SOME REFLECTIONS ON THE
AMERICAN REVOLUTION

BY ANDREW C. MCLAUGHLIN

THE SUBJECT assigned for this conference is within
the field of American history. I understand that this
field was decided upon, because this is the tercentenary of the great migration of Englishmen to
Massachusetts—one of the most striking and important movements of a people recorded in history. It
is not my purpose to dwell upon the significance
of that early settlement, or to recount the facts.
But, though speaking of the American Revolution,
I shall inevitably have in mind the principles these
founders of Massachusetts brought with them. The
most precious cargo of the "Arabella" was made up
of ideas and attitudes of mind.

The contacts and affiliations between the New
England colonists and the men of the earlier
seventeenth century in England who were opposing
the tyranny of the Stuarts did not end with the
migration to Boston. Someone has very wisely said
that America separated from Britain not in the
eighteenth century but in the seventeenth. An aphorism is always dangerous—it is almost sure to con-
tain as much falsehood as truth; but this aphorism
contains so much truth that its exaggeration can be
condoned. Certainly in some striking respects Amer-

ica, and notably New England, was the child of the
seventeenth century. If I may be allowed another
aphorism, I may say that in the revolution of the
eighteenth century Britain met in conflict the
England of the century before. It was difficult for
Parliamentarians to brush aside colonial arguments
in the days of Grenville and Townshend, unless they
ignored their own past. If I may indulge in another
dangerous sententious saying, I may well say that if
you look for precedents of American institutional
ideas, I mean essentially elementary ideas and
basic institutions, you will find some of them at
least in English history of the twenty years or thirty
before 1653. If we notice only the years from 1647 to
1653, and scan the documents prepared by the
Levellers and the men that gathered around the
campfires of the Ironsides we find there was one
cardinal thought: There must be unchanging law
as the basis of governmental power.

It is still not uncommon to speak of the American
Revolution as if it were the war; we keep our eyes
so firmly fixed upon the revolt and the struggle that
the nature of the whole movement is neglected.
In fact, we frequently speak as if the independence
of America was the only product worthy of serious
thought or of thought of any kind. Of course
independence, the breaking of the political ties
binding the colonies to a European country, was of
tremendous importance. But I am interested just

now in something else. I am interested in the ideas and principles of a period of history, and a creative period at that, and in the announcement and development of certain fundamental institutional principles. I am prepared to say that, if we take into consideration the extent of the influence of the principles and institutional forms upon the world at large, we shall be compelled to confess, despite all seemly modesty, that the men of that generation—some three million men scattered along the Atlantic coast on the edge of a continent—contributed more to the institutional structure of the world than did any other single generation in human history.

July fourth, 1787, Dr. Benjamin Rush made an address in Philadelphia containing the following passage, which directly referred to the tasks of the Federal Convention:

There is nothing more common than to confound the terms of American Revolution with those of the American War. The American War is over; but this is far from being the case with the American Revolution. On the contrary, nothing but the first act of the great drama is closed. It remains yet to establish and perfect our new forms of Government: and to prepare the principles, morals and manners of our citizens for these forms of Government after they are established and brought to perfection.

To the student of American constitutional history, the war was one conspicuous and important incident. But the development of institutions, the solving of problems, can be understood without much attention to actual hostilities. If we spend our time in seeking the causes of the conflict and in studying the conduct of battle, our study of institutional development seems to be disturbed rather than clarified. Let me try to make myself clear. A great deal of scholarly learning has been devoted to the years from the Stamp Act to the Declaration of Independence. The purpose of those investigations has been to understand why the colonists finally were ready to fight and how with arms in their hands they won independence. To find fault and not to applaud the critical study of the causes of the war and the events that followed its beginnings, would be silly indeed. But the constitutional historian has something else in mind—the emergence of institutions. With that for his object, begin where he may, he selects those events and pronouncements which explain, not the growing irritation of the colonies or the course of hostilities, but the creation of the United States as a political system; and in consequence he looks forward to a more distant goal than the Declaration or the Peace of Paris.

We may readily admit that the life of a nation or of a man does not consist of a series of separable factors and separable lines of conduct; but as a matter of plain fact we must select events and set aside those not appearing to lead us to our goal;

and it is the goal we wish to understand. This we do constantly in every piece of historical investigation; we are interested in any event or series of events not primarily for themselves alone; the isolated event (though of course no event is isolated) has no importance because of itself, but because it explains something else or fits into the picture we are trying to build for ourselves from the scattered fragments. Anything less is not history. So if you are intent upon discovering the emergence of American political institutions in order that you may know them, I propose to you this very simple but, in my judgment, absolutely necessary expedient: lift your eyes, if you begin your study with the mid-eighteenth century, and look forward for forty years or so to the formation of the United States.

For the student of our institutions the period of the American Revolution began with the distinct appearance of a constitutional problem; it ended when the solution of the problem was found. In selecting any period for study, the difficulty is to find a beginning; for we always find, in studying any movement, the necessity of understanding what preceded it; we are likely to be led farther and farther back. So, as I have already said, to understand the revolution of the eighteenth century we must know the rebellion and the revolution of the seventeenth, and to understand these we must know the development of the centuries preceding.

If we are not careful, we may find ourselves watching the landing of the English in Britain nearly fifteen hundred years ago, and be not content with the arrival of the "Arabella" on the coast of Massachusetts.

But for a moment let us be content with the appearance, the plain appearance, of the problem of imperial organization, and let us fix the date at 1754, when the Albany Plan of Union came from Franklin's prolific brain. The plan was not a device for curbing British rule, but a scheme for the organization of the British empire; and from that day on the actual problem was that of finding a method of holding together the parts of a widely spread empire and finding a satisfactory political system. The Plan was a precocious document, so precocious that we can see it in proper perspective only if we have in mind the work of the Constitutional Convention of 1787 and the perplexities with which the framers of the Constitution had to deal. We have thus a guiding thread through the countless events of that generation; in the processes of time a plan of imperial order was worked out; America found and founded a new type of body politic, the federal state, a state distinguished by the distribution of great sovereign powers between the constituent members on the one hand and the central government on the other.

So far I have been emphasizing only one thing, the desirability of fixing upon a period which was not broken into bits by wars or adventitious happenings, but had a certain unity of its own. If it began with 1754, it ended with the adoption of the federal constitution, which solved the problem of imperial order—and here again it may be said that the question whether the American people should form and maintain an integral continental system was the important salient question of modern history. But why should I take up so much of your time on this matter of fixing upon this period, as a single period? Because you cannot understand the founding of the United States if you do not connect the ideas of the two decades before the war with the constructive work that followed. The Revolutionary discussions that arose with the passage of the sugar act in 1764 and went on without ceasing, need for their understanding some appreciation of what resulted from the discussion and from the ideas which were put forth. Proposals and arguments of the Americans against the power of Parliament disclose a new meaning if we see in them the announcement of principles which were to be woven into the constitutional system of the United States. Furthermore, the problems of national integration and the establishment of a successful imperial system after 1776 were curiously like the problems of the old empire. In 1776 the problem of imperial order crossed the Atlantic; it became primarily an American problem.

31

The end of the American Revolution was, I have said, the formation of a new type of body politic—the federal or composite state. We may leave to the historical purists the question of whether the type was essentially new. If not without shadowy predecessors, it was, nevertheless, a contribution of America to world politics. No one now, wherever he may live, is quite unfamiliar with the principles of federalism. Federal states are scattered over the world. Nearly the whole of the two American continents is made up of federal states. Australia is a federal state; Germany is a federal state; Canada is a federal state; Russia is a federal state; the problem of finding a new system for India is associated with the problem of finding a suitable federal, as distinguished from a consolidated, system. This, I say, was a great contribution to the world; in the field of politics one of the greatest creations of all time. My suggestion to you is to appreciate the magnitude of the discovery.

In another paper, I have sought to show that in some of its elements, American federalism was the creature of the British Empire, that is to say the old empire within which the colonists had lived. Grant to the Fathers of 1787 the greatest wisdom imaginable, you will still be unable to believe that the American federal state was begotten in their minds without experience, without some principle or practice or habits leading them on. Let us reduce

32

this to its lowest possible terms: (1) federalism as a political system rests primarily on the distribution of powers among governments; (2) in the old British empire, there were many governments, and in practice, if not in law, each occupied its particular field; (3) the powers assigned to the national government under our Constitution, were, in an amazing degree, the powers commonly exercised by the central government of the old empire.

When we study the papers put forth by the colonists in the days before the war, if we bear in mind, not their sufficiency and validity as legal arguments against Britain, but their importance as expressions of beliefs and theories to be worked into our own constitutional structure, they have new interest, perhaps new meaning. Take, for example, Patrick Henry's famous resolutions of 1765; they proclaim two principles: (1) that taxation of the people by themselves or by persons chosen to represent them is the distinguishing characteristic of British freedom, without which the ancient constitution cannot subsist, and (2) that the colonists have uninterruptedly enjoyed the right of being governed by their own assembly "in the matter of their taxes and internal police." An argument concerning the legal validity of Henry's position is unnecessary; because all the argument in the world will not result in showing that he did not say what he did say. Among other things he was claiming for

3

Virginia within certain limits—within the field of taxation and the management of her internal affairs—an indefeasible share of the government as a constitutional portion of the empire. Whether he was technically right or technically wrong, for the moment does not affect me at all.

There was just no possibility of the appearance on the face of the earth of a constitution like that of the United States, in which powers of government were parcelled out among governments—and indeed parcelled out with rare discrimination—unless people could conceive that one governmental power could be distinguished from another power. Whether the colonies, as corporate entities, had authority within a limited field was one of two main questions of the American Revolution. The subject under discussion was, therefore, whether the fundamental principle of federalism was possible, whether the idea which was later institutionalized in the American Constitution was the essential principle of the old empire. Was the picture of an empire composed of integral parts, each possessing a portion, and only a portion, of governmental authority, the dream of madness or stupidity? This constitutes the chief meaning of Dickinson's "Farmers Letters." It is not a question of whether he was legally right or wrong when he pictured the old empire as one distinguished by the distribution of powers between colonies and mother country. You cannot envisage the establishment of federalism unless you distinguish between powers, or duties and responsibilities which can be separated one from the other, because they are of differing types. The Parliamentarians unfailingly pronounced as an axiom, as a fundamental logical principle which was beyond vulgar examination, the principle that government has all power or none; deny one power to government and you deny all. If this axiom is accepted, only a consolidated system of empire is within the realm of possibility. In one very important particular, therefore, the debate before the outbreak of hostilities was concerned with the very problem—I apologize for repetition—which the Americans solved in 1787; and Britain lost her colonies because she was unwilling or unable to see that distribution of powers could be recognized and established in the legal structure of the empire.

The American Revolution was characterized by legalism. The colonists might have admitted the legal authority of Britain to legislate as she chose, but have refused nevertheless to be bound by her laws; they might, in other words, have boldly proclaimed their intention to disobey, or to overthrow altogether, a legal government. This they did not openly do. Now the result was this: the Revolution was peculiarly conservative, in tone and temper. There were, it is true, riots and uprisings and tar and featherings, tea parties, and other doings of that sort; but there was no time when those whom we may consider leaders and framers of American thought, did not claim the possession of legal rights which were being encroached upon; they were not violators of law; they were defending the law. In a generation whose deeds were in the main constructive the importance of this quality of legalism cannot be over-estimated. Its deeds were constructive because its thinking was legalistic. These men were not, in their own minds, sweeping aside as totally base and worthless the structure of the empire, the teachings of English history, or the principles of English constitutionalism.

After the war began, there were various manifestations of what may be termed real revolutionary philosophy; the sort of philosophy which appeared in spectacular form in the French Revolution. Away with the past; let us begin over again and fashion a new system of society from the imaginings of our brains; let us renumber the years and rename the months. This philosophy, which impregnated the writings of Tom Paine, was essentially unhistorical, hence unconserving: "The palaces of kings are built upon the ruins of the bowers of paradise"; "Government like dress is a badge of lost innocence." From this it was only one step to a complete overthrow of institutions and practices of the past. But though this philosophy disturbed the orderly thinking of the masses, it was not triumphant. Over and over again, the Americans referred to the essentials of English constitutionalism and called upon Parliament to respect the products of English history. So we might ask: When is a revolution not a revolution? When its purpose is to save and protect, not to break down and scatter to the winds, principles and practices which the past has produced.

Much able and scholarly attention has been devoted to the question of the validity of the American arguments, and I do not wish to undervalue the scholarship or the importance of its product; it is of interest and importance in the history of the British empire. But if in announcing Parliamentary incompetence the theories of Henry or Dickinson or John Adams were technically unsound, that fact should not blind us to the nature and effect of what they said; and if the modern historian, like the Englishman of a century and more ago, holds the American positions to be untenable in law, such decision does not affect the actual course of events, the nature of the argument, its influence, or its disclosure of the character of the Revolution. The really important thing is what these men said, the implications of their words, and what they proceeded to do, not the legal validity of their argument.

Without any pretence of proposing an answer to the question of whether or not America's position, or, more properly, positions, can be upheld by British law or imperial law—if there were a law of the empire as distinguished from insular law—this may be admitted: the doctrines which the colonists were putting forth had not become actualized in Britain or in the empire; they had not received full institutional realization. The Americans therefore were claiming as their rights, claiming as part of the imperial order and of governmental authority, what in stark reality they were going to produce. That is why, though the Revolution was conservative, it was markedly constructive and progressive. If they asserted, in the days before the war, that the British empire was composite and not simple—that is to say, that the colonies were essentially integral parts of an integral empire, and that those parts had lawful authority within certain limits—they were actually announcing a form and fashion of empire which found legal and institutional reality in the federal constitution which they set up twelve years after argument had ended in war.

An attempt to reduce the Revolution to its lowest terms—and by that is meant, of course, to find if possible some single and salient principle which illustrates or permeates the whole and helps us to understand the whole—results in the conclusion you may well expect: the colonists denied the powers of Parliament; they bent their energies to a denial of Parliamentary omnipotence; they came toward the end to deny that Parliament had any authority at all. They denied that Parliament had all power; late in the day they began to assert that

Parliament had no power. They were driven by British argument to grasp one horn or the other of a dilemma—either Parliament had all power or none; and finally the colonists said it had none. There are, however indications that before the actual outbreak of hostilities they would have been content with what they believed to be the colonial share of empire. We do not distort America's position as a whole, if we select as the central doctrine the statement of the Massachusetts legislature of 1765, speaking of the authority of Parliament: "Bounds there undoubtedly are."

The colonists, whether they were announcing the right of the colonies as constituent parts of an empire or asserting their personal privileges as British subjects, set forth the principle of limited government. There again they were claiming, as already existing and as already their own, what in fact they were creating. When, for example, they announced the principle of no taxation without representation, they were not breaking entirely away from the precedents or theoretical principles of English constitutionalism; but the practices of British representation were humorously far from basing taxation on the will of the people at large. Britain had institutionalized the principle only to the extent of establishing the right of Parliament to grant to the crown the property of its subjects. In this respect, as in others, the colonies had outgrown the mother

country; they had made a nearer approach to a
system of equitable popular representation. The
Americans proclaimed, as an institutional fact, that,
to use a modern term, Britain had a fixed constitution, or, what is the same thing, a government of
limited scope. What are the two salient or cardinal
principles of the American constitutional system as
we know it today or as it was a hundred and forty
years ago? Plainly, first, the principle of federalism,
which means the distribution of powers among
independent governments; and, second, the principle, embodied in institutions, of limited government—government that can legally act only within
a prescribed field. These two principles, insisted
upon in the contest with Britain, became, when
fully made real, the contribution of America to
the political system of the modern world.

The belief that free government is limited government, a belief brought into play and intensified by
the experience of the years before the war, was
woven into the structure of our governmental
system, with the founding of state governments
bound by law. Freedom was consistent with legally
circumscribed authority and with that alone.
"For," said John Dickinson, "who are a free people?
Not those over whom government is reasonably and
equitably exercised but those who live under a
government so constitutionally checked and controlled that proper provision is made against its

40

being otherwise exercised." Probably no other single sentence can be found which will bring out so well the central thought of the American Revolution and the significance of what the Americans were to achieve. Freedom is not the right to do as one may choose, but is the right to live under law and not be subject to the whims, caprices, or arbitrary conduct of government. We have sometimes sought for the origins of one institutional principle and practice, which we call the power of a court to declare a legislative act void; to declare it to be no law at all. I have just given you—not the remote origin of this power, for, if we sought the real source, we should be carried far back into English history—but the cardinal doctrine of the American Revolution on which the power of courts rests today. Government, to act at all legally as government, must keep within the law. In the course of the preceding pages, I have spoken of the historical precedents or the more or less shadowy anticipations of American principles. Emphasize as we properly may the play of historical forces, the Americans—and this perhaps is their chiefest claim to fame—took doctrines, not entirely or at all new, theories, unembodied hopes, philosophic pronouncements, and made them actual and tangible in institutional forms and practices.

But how can it be said that a *revolution* is founded on *law* or is based upon legal or quasi legal theory? Simply by accepting the principle that, if the government acts beyond its legal authority, its commands are not binding; no one needs to obey. This doctrine or fundamental principle is often spoken of as if it were the result of a special revelation to the Fathers. But it is quite impossible to say how old that principle was when it was acted on by Revolutionary America and finally established in the American constitutional system. Certainly it was common in the compact or contract philosophy, now so much out of fashion; it was common also, in one form or another, in the half-religious half-political thinking of the Puritan ministers of New England, who believed and taught that no government could disregard the law of God. As early as 1692 Gershom Bulkeley declared no human law can be contrary to the law of nature and right reason, for an unreasonable law is a law against law, and unlawful authority is no authority.[1] In the famous pamphlet of Jonathan Mayew, issued a hundred years after the execution of Charles, he asserted that the king had "unkinged" himself.[2] These are but illustrations of a mode of thought based on Puritan seventeenth century thinking and

---

[1] Cf. Alice M. Baldwin, *The New England Clergy and the American Revolution* (Durham, N. C., Duke University Press, 1928).

[2] *A Discourse concerning unlimited Submission* (Boston, 1750; reprint Boston, 1818), p. 42. "All commands running counter to the declared will of the supreme legislator of heaven and earth are null and void; and therefore disobedience to them is a duty not a crime." *Ibid.*, p. 35.

carried down through the eighteenth century to the pronouncement of American independence. Strictly speaking, the right of revolution, if we adhere to the doctrine of the fathers and their forefathers, is not the right to overthrow government by force if the governmental conduct is disliked or has become irksome, but the right to resist, and, if it need be, put aside, a government which has transcended law and has therefore unkinged itself. It is not rebellion to resist a breach of the law.

Thomas Jefferson in the Declaration of Independence branded George III as a tyrant. It may be possible, without injuring anyone's patriotic feelings, to question the suitableness of that branding, if we mean by "tyranny" the conduct of a cruel and merciless ruler, loving to indulge in poisonings, spies, and poniards. Jefferson was not feeling very amiable towards George when he wrote his denunciation and his appeal to the opinion of mankind; but I judge that on the whole he was, nevertheless, living up to the philosophy so ably presented in the second paragraph of the immortal document. That philosophy was the philosophy of the social compact and of natural right: it was particularly the philosophy of John Locke, which had been repeated countless times, especially in New England, during the eighty years and more before Jefferson sat in the continental congress and heard Ben Franklin tell him the story of Thompson the hatter.

Tyranny, according to that philosophy, begins when law ends, if the law be transcended to the injury of the people; a tyrant is a ruler who goes beyond the law: "Wherever law ends, tyranny begins, if the law be transgressed to another's harm." We thus find in the Declaration itself the conspicuous American doctrine, underlying all American constitutionalism, that government is bound by law, and an act beyond the law is not law. The product of the Revolution was an institutionalized principle; courts were founded; they announced that an unconstitutional act is not law. To every one wishing to understand American institutions, I recommend the study of Locke's eighteenth chapter; and it is well also to remember that, though Jefferson knew Locke as one philosopher might know another, these doctrines had been handed down through the generations that had gone before.

In the earlier portion of my talk, I stressed the development of the concept of federalism, but I also pointed out that the central or pivotal position of Revolutionary argument was that the authority of Parliament was circumscribed. The colonists asserted that they lived under a limited government, not only because the colonies as such had a share in the empire and had their own prerogatives, but also because they were British subjects and had inherited principles of English liberty. In making this latter assertion they took refuge in the doctrine of natural rights, but those rights, we should notice carefully, were not some vague nebulous theories; they were, the colonists believed, embodied in the British constitution; they were part of English law. I may seem to be wandering off into strange pronouncements, if I say these men of a hundred and sixty years ago believed they were speaking the language and proclaiming principles of law, not abstract and disembodied philosophy or the fruits of a fervid imagination. When they quoted Lord Coke, to the effect that the common law would control acts of Parliament, they meant, of course, that the fundamental principles of right and justice embedded in the common law were beyond the profane touch of the most august legislative body in the world. Natural right and natural law, the law of God and of reason, the constitutional right of Englishmen to live under the care of an uncapricious, unself-willed government, were interlocked or meant the same thing. In the American mind the constitution of Britain was a fixed constitution, which, to use Sam Adams' words, "limits both sovereignty and allegiance." The constitution was fixed and unalterable in essentials, because it was grounded in natural God-given rights which are themselves unalterable; and God Himself, the sovereign of sovereigns, cannot disregard the limits of His own supreme and exacting holiness and justice. Whether we like the doctrines of natural right or not, the origins of our governmental system—as far as they can be seen in the outspoken ideas of men—are to be found in the belief in the unalterability of human rights which are not graciously bestowed by a kindly monarch.

The doctrine of natural rights, when thus explained, does not seem quite so airy and devoid of substance as it is so commonly supposed to be. But, once more, it makes no special difference to me as a student of constitutional history, whether this doctrine be silly or not. Foolish to us it may appear, but it was powerful; and if I were looking backward through the pages of history for one question which had for many centuries troubled the soul of man, I should not ignore this question: Are there not some things beyond the reach of government, some essential rights belonging to man which no ruler can lay his ruthless hands upon? Five hundred years before the Declaration of Independence, Thomas Aquinas wrote these words: "Every law framed by man bears the character of a law exactly to that point to which it is derived from the law of nature. But if at any point it is in conflict with the law of nature, it at once ceases to be a law, it is a mere perversion of law." When I see the Supreme Court of the United States casting aside as no law an act of a state legislature because it is contrary to the fundamental principles of right and justice which they find safeguarded in the due process of law by a clause of the fourteenth amendment, or when I find one justice, giving the opinion of the Court in the Insular Cases, some thirty years ago, asserting, as a primary rule of law, that Congress in managing our colonies is restricted by those pronouncements in the Constitution which are intended to protect natural rights, I begin to doubt whether the much contemned natural-rights theory is long since dead, though it has been cast into the discard by the philosophers of the present and the preceding generation. And when I find a litigant in court standing upon his rights, with no presumption, either on the bench or at the bar, of any obligation on his part to show that such rights are the gift of government, but with the assumption that he has rights which government is founded to protect, my doubts are strengthened; and I am inclined to think that, foolish as this old time-worn doctrine may be, it not only was used in the American Revolution but also powerfully affected our constitutional system. But my main assertion here is that America institutionalized the old idea. I do not find it a very great leap from Thomas Aquinas to the Supreme Court of the United States in 1930, casting out legislation because, as the justices would say, the act in question was unfair, unjust, and an intrusion on the right of the individual litigant at the bar of justice.

Let us now turn to the Declaration of Independence and con the words of its early sentences, said by a clever speaker of a later day, himself an artist in dialectics, to be filled with glittering generalities. The first significant thing about the Declaration is that it was issued at all; the Americans did not simply grasp scythe and flintlock to fight their way to liberty. And perhaps even more striking is the appeal to the opinions of mankind, as if there were any mankind to be appealed to, any conscience of the world, or as if there were a conscious and conscientious world, that would not be shocked and amazed by a revolution against authority no matter how cleverly the cause was presented in happily chosen words.

The statement of the Declaration most commonly criticised is that all men are created equal. In the latest book on constitutional problems which I have taken in my hand, can be found an outcry against the absurdity and the iniquity of this false announcement. Men, we are told, are not equal; how great, then, is the folly to proclaim what is untrue and is demoralizing in practice because it is not true. Jefferson, however, was not altogether lacking in brains; he was writing an appeal to the opinions of mankind and one which he hoped would express the sentiments of the American people. Could he have believed it an axiom among men that every man was as wise, as strong, as sober, as industrious, as trustworthy as every other? Of course not. Did he advocate full and equal participation in government,

48

universal suffrage, equality of temporal possessions, and all the other equalities you can think of? And, at that place and that time, did he advocate theories of government, which the men who were then setting up state governments were prepared to disregard? The words were perhaps unhappily chosen. The language of the Virginia bill of rights was somewhat better, "all men are by nature equally free and independent"; and this means all men are equal in a state of nature; before governments are established, before rulers are set up, no one is the superior of another. How then did it come about that one man or one set of men came to have authority, to make rules for the conduct of the rest and to punish them for misconduct? That, in fact, was no new question. In the decades and centuries gone by, men had asked themselves the same question. Originally men were equal; they existed in a state of nature, in possession of God-given rights, with no umpire, no guide, no authority, but only their own reasons and their own individual strength. In setting up government they disposed of this equality; they subjected themselves to authority; not to an absolute authority but only to one under obligation to respect the rights which the people had not surrendered. To say that this theory is utterly unsound does not help us at all. It was unhistorical, as we use the word historical, for history is an account of actual facts or the sequence of facts

49

4

themselves. Historical thinking is realistic, and the natural-rights doctrines are artificial. In reality, however, if we look into history, as I am attempting to do, we find as an *historical* fact, that men did deal in the artificial. The difference between facts and artifacts, struck off for purposes of political argument, is quite plain to us; but even in the days of Edward Gibbon and Adam Smith, artificiality had not been abjured for the realism of history.

The doctrine of the Declaration is, therefore, not that all men are in all respects equal *after* governors and rulers are set up, but that they were equal originally; and they set up government over themselves, a government with powers and with the right to demand obedience, the right to command, provided the government did not transcend certain limits, the limits which guarded the fundamental unalienable rights of the subjects. How, men asked, did this inequality come to be, an inequality legal as long as its primary foundations were respected? One gets tired of hearing the Declaration quietly ridiculed on the ground that it proclaimed the absolute and complete equality of all men in every particular, or even the absolute right of all men equally to participate in government. Strictly speaking, the doctrine of the Declaration in this particular would have been consistent with an intent to set up a monarchy, for the words were used only to remind King George and mankind, that there were limits on the legal authority of monarchs. There were limits to the obedience due from the subject.

The second paragraph of the Declaration of Independence is a remarkable piece of condensation. In some two hundred and fifty words Jefferson condensed the whole argument of Locke's famous essay on government. Presumably he did not have the essay with him; he must have known it thoroughly; one small portion is given word for word, and Locke's critical positions are given with accuracy. This reasoning was of course not peculiar to Locke. Some of it probably—though I know of no documentary proof of the fact—was inherited even from feudalism, with its essential idea of a contractual relationship, and from the principle that the vassal was not the slave of his overlord, against whom he could quote the binding character of feudal law. Some of it was gathered, as the Revolution of 1688 shows, from the coronation oath of the king. Some of it was found in the theology and the ecclesiastical polity of the Puritan seventeenth century. Some of it presumably came from the age-long controversy between Church and State. Much of it was found in the doctrines of philosophic writers. But we can pay special attention to Locke, because we know his volume was referred to constantly by the men of the American Revolution, and because we know, and do not merely surmise, that

Jefferson must have been well acquainted with Locke's second essay.

To protect natural and inalienable rights "governments are instituted among men, deriving their just powers from the consent of the governed." Possibly Jefferson had in mind, by "consent of the governed," continuing consent through representation; but the fundamental idea is that government originates in agreement; it is not self-originating. The most important word in the Declaration is "deriving"; governmental authority is derivative authority. The words seem to sum up the long contest between the divine right of people and the divine right of kings. Accept one or the other of these conflicting doctrines or postulates and you must end in inevitable conclusions. The defenders of the divine right of kings scorned the idea that power is derived from people; government, though for argument's sake they sought its origin in the heaven, was possessed of inherent, intrinsic, inborn power as distinguished from derived power. If you deny this inherent and indigenous quality, you sweep away the argument and the conclusion; you must accept the doctrine that government derives its authority from the consent of the governed. I have been seeking the elementary ideas of the Revolution and the Declaration; and again though I have pointed to many things as if each were the most essential, I am inclined to fasten now upon this announcement of the derivative character of government. You may be able to find, though I cannot, something more characteristic or more descriptive of American constitutionalism than this, but I doubt it. You may be able to think out a position from which you may win your battle against the theory of the divine right of government, a government which has inherent authority—you may perchance find a position more definite than the doctrine that men existed before government and bestowed upon government its authority; but the historical fact is that this position was taken by the men of the seventeenth century and by the men of the American Revolution.

Let us take another phrase or two of the many that flowed from Jefferson's facile pen and let us content ourselves. He faced, as did Locke, the objection raised by all defenders of the divine right of kings and absolute government, that the whole theory of those opposing kingly power rested on the right to disobey; you cannot, said the divine-right men, rest government on disobedience; it must rest on the duty and the obligation to obey; government without authority is a contradiction in terms; obedience is necessary for the very existence of government. I wish I could show you the clever way in which Locke met this objection; but after all Jefferson presented it in few words and with remarkable cogency, and in doing so used some of Locke's own expressions:

Prudence, indeed, will dictate that Governments long established should not be changed for light and transient causes; and accordingly all experience hath shown that mankind are more disposed to suffer, while evils are sufferable, than to right themselves by abolishing the form to which they are accustomed. But when a long train of abuses and usurpations, pursuing invariably the same object evinces a design to reduce them under absolute despotism, it is their right, it is their duty, to throw off such government and provide new guards for their future security.

The right of revolution, according to the progressives of the seventeenth century and the men of the American Revolution, was the right to oppose illegal government. How cleverly Jefferson stated the principles! He did not content himself with proclaiming the right to revolt; he spoke of the power and authority of the people to set up governments; he had in mind the constructive and reconstructive work demanded by the situation.

The theory of the Declaration and the essence of the Revolution were not confined to the right to revolt against arbitrary and hence illegal authority; the essence is found in the assertion of the right not only to abolish or alter governments, but to institute new governments. Well, what was the Revolution? I may have already proposed several answers, but now I say: it was the transformation of colonies into

54

self-governing commonwealths. The transformation was made, in greater or less degree, strictly in conformity with the theory that the people were the source of power. In some cases this theory was carried out with meticulous adherence to the essentials—with scrupulous adherence as exact as anything could be, short of literal dissolution of society into its component atoms before the reorganization of a new political society and a new government. As far as actual method was concerned, the people of Massachusetts and New Hampshire followed consciously, accurately, and systematically the theory of the Declaration and the advice of Adams that the people should follow the instruction of the "wisest writers" and erect the whole structure with their own hands. They were somewhat more conscious than were the people of other states of the necessity of so moving that theories were made plain and tangible. They found the thoroughly correct method for the manifestation of the principle that government is the creature of the people. The American people discovered and put into use the representative constitutional convention, the basic American institution.

Let us not sneer at the fantasies of compact philosophy and the doctrine of natural rights, i.e., the doctrine that men may set up government, which must protect them, or the doctrine, closely allied, if it be not the same, that government is bound by law. In natural law and social compact you may find, if you so desire, nothing but the vagaries of the human intellect; but you will see that the Americans did discover a method of establishing government on the basis of popular power; and in the long course of history I don't think you will find any greater political achievement. Certainly that discovery or invention can stand unabashed even in the presence of the principle and method of representation, to which possibly may be accorded essential primacy among occidental political institutions. So, as I said a short time ago, the American Revolution was constructive rather than destructive; and if it did nothing more than produce the constitutional convention, as an answer to the age-long question, "How can people, mere people, establish government?", that answer would give distinction to the Revolution. The "right of revolution" found its consummation in the methods and institutions, whereby, without an appeal to heaven, to use Locke's words, government and the state can be reorganized.

In the course of the preceding pages I have sought among other things to make connection between the thinking and the character of the seventeenth century and the birth of the United States. In the space at my disposal I could give little more than indications or hints of such connection. One more word is necessary. I have just spoken of America's discovering the convention as an instrument in the process of constitution-making. There has recently been some interesting discussion concerning the town in Massachusetts, where the fully developed idea concerning the constitutional convention first found full expression a little over a hundred and fifty years ago. I believe the evidence favors bestowal of the honor upon Concord. But these ideas seem to get new significance if we turn to the proposals made by the radicals in England, one hundred and thirty years or so before the meeting of the justly famous Massachusetts convention—and we may ask again, as we often do, whether there is anything new under the sun. I read from a document prepared by the Independents and Levellers at the height of the great Rebellion of the mid-seventeenth century.

That some persons be chosen by the Army to represent the whole Body; and that the well-affected in every County (if it may be) chuse some persons to represent them: And those to meet at the Head-Quarters.

That those persons ought not to exercise any Legislative power, but onely to draw up the foundations of a just Government, and to propound them to the well-affected people in every County to be agreed to: Which Agreement ought to be above Law; and therefore the bounds, limits, and extent of the peoples Legislative Deputies in Parliament, contained in the Agreement to be drawn up into a formall contract to be mutually signed by the well-affected people and their said Deputies upon the dayes of their Election respectively. . . .[4]

[4]Quoted in T. C. Pease, *The Leveller Movement*, p. 261.

Now, having gone back to the mid-seventeenth century, a hundred and thirty years before the founding of Massachusetts' constitution, let us move forward from that founding nearly one hundred years to quote, as an evidence of the historical longevity of certain old-fashioned doctrines, the words of the Supreme Court of the United States: "When one becomes a member of society, he necessarily parts with some rights or privileges, which, as an individual not affected by his relations with others, he might retain. 'A body politic,' as aptly defined in the preamble of the Constitution of Massachusetts, 'is a social compact by which the whole people covenant with each citizen, and each citizen with the whole people, that all shall be governed by certain laws for their own good.'" This, the Court goes on to say, "does not confer power upon the whole people to control rights which are purely private."[5] If this is not a recognition of the theory of the compact or contract origin of government and the theory of natural rights, we shall have to find other words to express exactly the same idea.

Possibly I have made clear certain facts that did not need clarification—you cannot understand the American Revolution without understanding the seventeenth century, and you can't understand the nineteenth century without studying the principles

[5] *Munn* v. *Illinois* (1876) 94 U. S. 113, 124.

and ideas of the eighteenth. Furthermore, a truism in historical criticism, you cannot understand what men meant by what they said, unless you refrain from imposing upon their words a connotation foreign to the men that uttered them. Such an imposition, which is an abomination to the student trained in historical criticism, has been specially common in the interpretation of the Declaration. May I also in conclusion repeat another principle of historical research? The searcher in the field of constitutional history need not be continually and uniformly bent upon finding whether a position taken by one side or the other in formal argument and at a crisis is technically sound or not; the position he thinks unsound may be the really creative and productive one. If the Americans one hundred and sixty years ago were wrong in law, according to your opinion, nevertheless your opinion does not alter the course of history.

Some portions of what I have said may sound strange in the ears of the learned; for it may be said that I am defending the doctrine of natural rights and of social compact, the crippled if not deceased children of a false political philosophy. But I do not wish to be misunderstood; my purpose is not to defend and not to attack, but to propose briefly the desirability of understanding those doctrines and of noticing the way in which they were used. We should see how much these doctrines or their remnants influenced thinking on constitutional matters during many decades after 1776. And among my assertions you will find the statement that the colonists believed they were announcing law, thinking in the terms of English constitutionalism, and further proclaiming that an act of a legislature beyond law is not a law at all—surely one principle which we cannot consider antiquated or buried and sleeping with the "rude forefathers" of our constitutional system. That is the central principle of American constitutional law; we find its beginnings in the assertions of the compact philosophy, and also in the principles of English liberty. As illustrative of this last point may I once more quote Locke, who shows us the connection between this theory of compact and the principle of limited government, the principle which the Americans institutionalized:

The commission, or command of any magistrate where he has no authority, being as void and insignificant as that of any private man, the difference between the one and the other being that the magistrate has some authority so far and to such ends, and the private man has none at all; for it is not the commission but the authority that gives the right of acting, and against the laws there can be no authority. (Section 206.)

But yet it is to be observed that though oaths of allegiance and fealty are taken to him, it is not to him as supreme legislator, but as supreme executor of the law made by a joint power of him with others, allegiance being nothing but an obedience according to law, which when he violate, he has no right to obedience, nor can claim it otherwise than as the public person vested with the power of law. . . . But when he quits this representation, this public will, and acts by his own private will, he degrades himself, and is but a single private person without power and without will; the numbers owing him no obedience but to the public will of the society. (151.)

He that hath authority to seize my person in the street may be opposed as a thief and a robber if he endeavours to break into my house to execute a writ, notwithstanding that I know he has such a warrant and such a legal authority as will empower him to arrest me abroad. And why this should not hold in the highest, as well as in the most inferior magistrate, I would gladly be informed. (202.)

I have been trying to speak connectedly of the American Revolution, of its association with the legal and philosophical theories of earlier times and of the importance of our appreciating the influence of those ideas on the essentials of American constitutionalism. But when all is said we find that system resting on one main principle: government is subject to law; anyone high or low breaking the law cannot claim obedience; an officer without authority can be held guilty of trespass upon individual rights; the right of revolution is the right to refuse obedience to illegal acts. The quotations from Locke just given show the connection between some of the elementary principles of the common law and the underlying principles of American constitutionalism: Every man is responsible for his own wrongs; an officer trespassing without legal authority upon another's rights is personally responsible for his conduct, for only law can justify interference with private freedom of action. This legal principle constitutes the everyday method by which those in authority, and therefore government itself, can be kept within the pale of assigned constitutional power.

ARE WE BETTER THAN OUR ANCESTORS?

ARE WE BETTER THAN OUR ANCESTORS?

BY DIXON RYAN FOX

THE AIR of Massachusetts is thick this year with
history. The shifting sands, the breeze-swept,
wooded hills, old thoroughfares of trade, the wheels
of industry, all seem to murmur of experience, of
the great tradition of the old Bay State. "There are
no dead," said Maeterlinck; now and again upon
occasions such as this we feel the past, the living past,
that urges or restrains our daily purpose, makes one
course hard, another easy, as if unseen spirit fingers
entwined with ours to lead us into paths that this
persuasive past has made appropriate. We realize
suddenly the persisting force of a tradition. Progress
is not made by abject yielding to such guidance,
the manner of conservatism; but intelligence must
know tradition if it is to choose along what way,
among several, progress can be most effectively
achieved. We read history to know ourselves.

Most men enjoy the thought that they are heritors
of the past, especially the local past; newcomers feel
more comfortable as they adopt the background of
the place, and today a multitude whose ancestors
were Irish, Polish, French, Italian, Portuguese are
celebrating with full gusto the tradition of John
Winthrop's Boston. Not infrequently, indeed, an
individual or a family migrates to a spot of earth,

not because of economic opportunity alone, or legal privileges or physical comfort in themselves, but because the tradition of the place is irresistibly congenial. Social life is made the richer by the memories that lie behind it. "To abstract the mind from all local emotion," wrote Dr. Johnson, "would be impossible, and would be foolish if it were possible."

But if local tradition sets its hand upon us it may prove an exacting master. When Marc Antony declared that the evil men do lives after them and that the good oft lies interred with their bones, he spoke contrary to all experience. Ancestor worship is not confined to the Chinese. The haze of retrospection has a magnifying quality. It is a favorite thesis with the moralists that the times generally grow worse, and this attitude is nothing new; the Code of Hammurabi, written nearly forty-three hundred years ago, begins, familiarly: "In the good old days . . ." Youth is constantly exhorted to emulate the virtue and the enterprise that so signally distinguished the great-great-grandfathers, but in this advice there is usually a plaintive overtone of hopelessness; it is too much to expect. Cotton Mather wrote his greatest work to serve this purpose. In many a pulpit, on many a celebration rostrum, during these eventful days in Massachusetts, we are contrasted with the Puritans of 1630 to our grievous disadvantage. The defeatist note creeps in;

it is not likely, we are told, that we can ever equal them.

Standing here amid these hills we cannot well compare the folk of Hampshire county with their predecessors of three hundred years ago; the red man stalking game through shadowed forests according to immemorial custom, touches our history but is scarcely of it. Then came the founding of this town, a thrice told tale that will ever stir the blood of its successive generations. "Plantations," wrote Lord Bacon, meaning the settlements of pioneers, "Plantations are amongst ancient, primitive and heroic works." The seventeenth-century scene in Hadley, as we see it now, was picturesque—painted savages and the sack and pillage of race war, outlaw regicides revered as tools of God and harbored against the long arm of the Stuarts, to say nothing of the hideous iniquities of witchcraft, and the awful drama of Hell and Paradise so vividly unfolded from the lofty pulpit. The eighteenth century with its steady conquest of the wilderness, the tread of marching feet as men went out to clear the continent of Frenchmen, the rumble of martial drums that sounded the birth cry of a nation—all this is part of the American tradition, just as our own life day by day, hour by hour, slips into its procession. But granted that destiny trudged on beside the founders, colonial social life was for long so elementary that it scarcely serves for a comparison with our own. After the Revolution, however, there is no mistaking that we have before us a mature and homogeneous community in the eastern parts of America, a community with well marked principles and habits.

It may be, then, a profitable enterprise to set side by side in some respects the outlook of that generation at the beginning of the nineteenth century with our own at the beginning of the twentieth. Direction is determined by two successive points. We may be able to detect some trend and, if there has been change, to test it in the terms of progress.

In some concerns the answer is so obvious that the question seems unnecessary, if not absurd. The technique of living has changed more in these hundred years than it had in all historic time before. As far as carrying persons, goods and thoughts from one place to another was concerned, Herodotus would have been at home along with the other foreign travelers who visited America in 1800. Except the compass and the telescope there was no device of travel or communication which he would not have found familiar. Today man has almost conquered distance. It is a question if the Hadley farmer of that time, mud-bound in spring as he was each year, would not be as much astonished at the concrete highways of the present as at the incredibly fleet machines that dart along their surface. Seated by your fireside you can hear a word as soon as it is whispered on the other side of the Atlantic; men have now flown across that great expanse of ocean almost in a day; we have a well-based expectation that we soon shall see across it. Space is almost obsolete. So habituated are we to all such improvements that what must yet be done to perfect these achievements we know will be done; with such infinitude of premises, prophecy has scarce need of faith. Heating his home with automatic furnaces and cooling it with mechanical refrigeration, man has almost abolished the seasons. To conquer night he needs only press a button. The world's work is done not with muscle but with ingenuity, an ingenuity which has made possible a consumption of materials by the humblest that would have aroused the envy of great kings in years gone by.

All this is quite too manifest for much elaboration. But the conservers of tradition and the moralists brush it all aside. Ill fares the land, they warn us, where instruments accumulate and purposes decay. Admitting that we all now live like kings, do we live like better men? With tedious insistence they inquire if we have not raised a Frankenstein that we cannot control, and hint that life was nobler and, indeed, more lovely in the days before the ministry of the machine. Evidence, not intuition, must supply the answer. Probably a definite and certain verdict could never be reached, yet briefly sampling the multifarious records of that other day may yield some sense of tendency.

It has escaped the attention of historians, as historians, that half the race are women. What was the position of woman in Massachusetts a century ago? The single woman had, as in England, substantially the same legal rights as men, but the married woman was civilly dead. Neither her earnings, her personal property, nor the income from it were legally under her control. In the latter twenties Elizabeth Cady ran into her father's office to show her young lawyer cousin the new coral necklace and bracelets she had received for Christmas. "Now," he answered teasingly, "if in due time you should be my wife those ornaments would be mine; I could take them and lock them up, and you could never wear them except with my permission. I could exchange them for a box of cigars, and you could watch them evaporate in smoke." No wife could make a contract; none, therefore, could enter business. A woman could not legally be treasurer of her own sewing society in this state before 1840, unless some man were responsible for her. The first onslaught on the age-old common law in these respects in this country came in Judge John Fine's law of 1848 in the State of New York on the property rights of married women. But married or single, women had no participation in the making of such laws or any others; few women alive in 1830 would ever cast a vote for state or national officials at the polls of Massachusetts.

Men had rights, it seems, but women had only duties; and apparently no one raised a protest. But these political and civil disabilities will astonish our children more than us, within whose memory they have, some of them, been abolished. Far more impressive were the social inequalities. Those who feel that there are remnants of injustice in the circumscription of the present sphere of women should imagine themselves in the Massachusetts of a hundred years ago.

Girls were schooled in fundamentals, but seldom much beyond. At the beginning of the nineteenth century there were forty-eight academies in Massachusetts, only three of which were maintained for girls, though a few besides admitted them in limited number along with the boys. Girls were not expected to keep the pace of their brothers. Timothy Dwight, once a citizen of nearby Northampton, informs us that, "the reading of girls is regularly lighter than that of boys. Where the standard of reading for boys is set too low, that for girls will be proportionately lowered. Where boys investigate books of sound philosophy, and labour in mathematical and logical pursuits, girls read history, the higher poetry, and judicious discourses in morality and religion. When the utmost labour of boys is bounded by history, biography, and the pamphlets of the day; girls sink

down to songs, novels and plays." The reverend
president sets this forth without a comment; it was
all apparently according to God's good plan.

But here and there was a prophetic voice calling
for reform. Dr. J. S. J. Gardiner, of Boston, believed
that girls in 1809 were retarded not by lack of wit,
but by lack of opportunity. Boys were allowed to
stay in real school acquiring discipline of mind.
"Girls, on the other hand, of the same age, are
employed in the mere manual exercise of sprigging
muslin, painting flowers, and fingering a musical
instrument; employments comparatively frivolous,
and little connected with intellectual improvement.
If [in addition] to these trifling attainments they can
dance gracefully and prattle French, they are
deemed by their injudicious friends all-accom-
plished. . . ." Girls, he said, learned only for
display, and this he properly deplored. Let women
learn elementary mathematics and the grammar of
the English and the Latin tongues, let them form a real
acquaintance with great writings, and see what
happens. "Only lay a solid foundation and you
may raise on it a superstructure as airy as you
please." But at least two generations were to pass
before his excellent ideal was realized. Twenty
years after he delivered this address, the first
public examination of a girl in geometry was held in
a New York school; the clergy prophesied that if
such things went on the family bonds were sure to

be dissolved. The credit for the first appropriation of state funds for girls' seminaries belongs to Emma Willard and New York in 1819, but it was nearly twenty years afterward that the first woman's college was organized with mighty effort at Mount Holyoke.

Girls grew up without intellectual opportunity, but we are not to think that society was unconcerned as to their thought and action. In the reading especially provided for them they were told the secrets of success. "Be inconspicuous," wrote one author included in the widely circulated *Lady's Pocket Library*, published in 1793. "One of the chief beauties in a female character," wrote another in the same collection, "is that modest reserve, that retiring delicacy, which avoids the public eye, and is disconcerted even at the gaze of admiration. . . . Wit is the most dangerous talent you can possess." Whether the heroines of fiction produced the ethereal, clinging, delicate young ladies in real life or vice versa, one cannot say, but certainly they flourished in polite America at the beginning of the nineteenth century. "With the character of a Christian woman," observed the sapient author of the *Young Ladies' Own Book*, "nothing, methinks, can better correspond, than a propensity to melt into affectionate sorrow." Praising a young and elegant person he had met, a distinguished traveler finds additional attraction in the delicate state of her

73

health. Intellectually woman was to be as incurious as possible, especially with respect to religious truths certified by orthodoxy. "Never perplex yourself about such as you do not understand, but treat them with silent and becoming reverence"; this was the advice of Hannah More, an English moralist universally admired in this country.

The American woman of the early nineteenth century was a model of domestic virtue, but commentators sighed that early marriages, the bearing and the care of children, and the rigor of farm life made most of them seem old at thirty. As to the proper wifely attitude there was no question. St. Paul had settled that long since: "Wives submit yourselves unto your own husbands as unto the Lord." St. Peter had said the same thing, though he had charged husbands to be tender, "giving honor unto the wife as to the weaker vessel." There were few pastors in the state who would have questioned this. Man was not created for woman, but woman was for man. An eminent Calvinist in Philadelphia reviewed the qualities that should adorn the matrimonial union—"intelligence and generosity of temper on the part of the husband, meekness and complacency on the part of the wife." "Where want of congeniality impairs domestic comfort," admonished another authority, "the fault is generally chargeable on the female side; for it is for woman, not for man, to make the sacrifice especially in indifferent matters. . . . Her weakness is an attraction, not a blemish." Meekly forgiving, she must accept a double standard in sex conduct, and realize, as one lady said, that "What among men is reputed a venial fault, is an absolute crime with us."

Woman's place, it scarcely need be said, was in the home. Mary Wollstonecraft's proposals to the contrary were greeted with derision and disgust. A poet averred:

> Dame Nature tells us Mary's rights are wrong
> Her female freedom is a Syren Song.

The pulpit answered in the same strain: "The God of nature has raised everlasting barriers against such wild speculations; . . . to urge them is to renounce reason, to contradict experience, to trample on the divine authority and to degrade the usefulness, the honor, the real enjoyment of the female sex." Woman must accept this gracefully; she should prefer a second part in life's concert; when she attempted to lead the band her soft notes became scrannel and discordant by being strained beyond their pitch. The professions were closed. The first woman to receive a medical degree in the United States was Elizabeth Blackwell of Geneva Medical College in western New York in 1849, but most people thought her "either mad or bad." She died but twenty years ago. There was no woman lawyer in this state or any other until the sixties. In 1840 Miss Martineau found but seven employments open here to women; today there are scarcely seven that are not. There was no way that a woman could engage in organized religion or philanthropic work except as a member of the Female Cent Society in support of foreign missions and one or two others like the Female Asylums to make orphan girls into household servants. The woman's club was unknown to the woman of 1830; destiny reserved it for her granddaughters.

It would be a serious mistake to think that America was backward among the nations of Christendom with respect to woman's status. Travelers agreed that she had more freedom here than elsewhere. We are comparing times, not nations; and it seems an ineluctable conclusion that the feminine half of America is vastly better off today than it was in 1830. There is nothing that she did then that she cannot do now, while alternatives in this new age stand waiting on every side.

It was the dictum of a Harvard scientist of sixty years ago, John Fiske, that as life rises in the scale of evolution more and more attention is paid to the period of infancy. It will be instructive for a few brief moments to compare the Massachusetts of the early nineteenth century with the Massachusetts of today in its care for childhood. Its system of tax-supported schools was the model of the world. "The noble example of New England," said Frances

Wright in 1829, "has been imitated by other states, until all not possessed of common schools blush for the popular remissness."

We must remember at the start, however, that the legal standards of the state had fallen in 1789, when towns were relieved of the obligation to maintain grammar schools until they had two hundred families instead of one hundred specified in 1647, and they had been lowered again in 1824; this signified an effort to have the law conform to practice. It must be remembered, too, that the six-months elementary school required by law might be a moving school with two months in one corner of the town and like terms in the others, the rudimentary "deestricts."

But more important than the law by which such schools were ordered is the quality of the learning that was there maintained. As streams can rise no higher than their sources one looks first at the teaching personnel. Women were employed but sparingly except in summer terms, when the big boys were away in the fields at work. The winter term, beginning the Monday after Thanksgiving, needed a master who could beat such rebels into outward order. Oftentimes this was the limit of his competence, if, indeed, he could achieve that. Over three hundred Massachusetts schools were broken up in the year 1837 because the teachers could not keep school. Many masters were itinerant foreigners, especially Irishmen, given to drinking and gambling. We are told that in a Connecticut town in 1822 six out of fifteen applicants were rejected because they could not count in the larger numbers or indicate the four fundamental processes in cyphering, and yet they came well recommended from towns where they had taught. It is no wonder that they frequently skipped fractions.

In Boston, in 1800, the public school masters got $666.66 yearly, but this was the highest standard in the country, and small communities could raise but a small portion of this impressive sum. When a college student was secured to teach a winter term the district school was fortunate; but this remained in most towns an infrequent blessing.

The textbooks had high purpose. A reader, for example, was presented on its title page as "Calculated to eradicate vulgar prejudice and rusticity of manners; inform the understanding; rectify the will; purify the passions; direct the minds of youth to the pursuit of proper objects; to facilitate their reading, writing, and speaking the English language, with elegance and propriety." If it did all this the book was worth its price, but reports of teaching methods raise our doubts. Out of long experience in New England schools, a teacher testified that the ideal in teaching elementary literature was to have the scholar read both loud and fast. He says that he began to write compositions in his twelfth winter in

78

school; he was first taught writing at the age of nine, arithmetic at the age of twelve. Speaking of a popular textbook he points out that faith and memory were all that were demanded of the novice. The master *heard* the lessons. Pike's arithmetic, which that generation largely favored, the modern scholar finds only a Pandora's box of disconnected rules, many of them touching processes the pupil could never conceivably have occasion for in life; it appealed exclusively to memory and not at all to reason. Daniel Adams' *Geography* (1818) was widely used; Part I consisted of ten pages of geographical names to be used as spelling lessons, Part II of fifty pages of facts to be memorized verbatim, and Part III of "A Description of the Earth . . . to be read aloud by the class." A writer in the *Literary Magazine* thought that civics might be taught to older children. Anticipating the objection that they might not feel attracted to it, he answered with impatience: "Naturally, they pay little attention to learning of any kind; they should be obliged to learn this as they are other things." There was no John-Deweyism here, no enervating doctrine that a child should follow lines of interest in developing his knowledge. Pestalozzi was a novelty in 1830, and reasoning for children a matter of cautious experiment by pioneers. The child as a subject of scientific study was just emerging. Up to then children were little men and women in responsibilities as well as dress. They must put their thought on life, death and the great hereafter. Little readers of one primer spelled it out in these words:

> Our days begin with trouble here
> Our life is but a span;
> And cruel death is always near
> So frail a thing is man.

Great minds came up from the little red schoolhouse, but few who know the typical educational process of a century ago would deny us a sense of progress in that most important field.

Play was tolerated as a human frailty in most places, though not in all. When the original bishops of the Methodist church founded their school in Maryland near the close of the eighteenth century they spoke clearly on this subject: "The students shall be indulged with nothing which the world calls play. Let this be observed with strictest nicety; for those who play when they are young will play when they are old." Sports were usually enervating, thought the *Christian Examiner* in 1830; one could seldom pray for the blessings of God upon entering them. "Such useless, but fashionable amusements, as religion forbids," observed the *Massachusetts Missionary Magazine* some years before, "are perhaps the direct paths of gradual and easy descent to the grosser vices. They are called innocent amusements. . . . [But] their usual tendency is to dissipate the mind, and make it impatient of useful labor, and of religious duties. . . . And are such amusements fit to be recommended to immortal youth, who must shortly appear before the tribunal of God? . . . Then forbid the prodigal waste of golden days in youth; and let the great doctrines of religion furnish you with adequate sanction to enforce your salutary prohibitions." Leisure was scarcely respectable at any period of life. Frank Forester recalling his first days in America, about a hundred years ago, says that any lawyer seen skirting the town with a fishing rod in his hand, risked, if he did not forfeit, his professional reputation. But a tendency to play had to be watched especially among the young. A generation of Calvinists that read Proverbs with attention earnestly hoped that little sluggards would go to the ant for their example. Work was a universal good.

Secretary Hamilton recommended manufactures to America on the ground that it would give employment to the idle hands of little children. How excellent was the condition in England! "Of the number of persons employed in the cotton manufactories of Great Britain, it is computed that four-sevenths nearly are women and children, of whom the greatest proportion are children, and many of them of a tender age." Patriotic Americans should strive to reproduce this here. It was a proud day when, in 1824, the *Commercial Advertiser* could

6

announce that Mr. Ayres of Ithaca, who manufactured imitation Leghorn hats, would soon employ "one hundred females, some of whom are not more than eight years of age." One comes upon advertisements for lively boys aged eight. In 1810 Alvah Crocker, who was in time to figure as a leading manufacturer of Massachusetts, was a little boy of eight working twelve hours each day for his wage of twenty-five cents. In 1825 a committee of the Massachusetts Senate saw no reason to interfere with such conditions. A generation was to live and die before this state assumed the lead in labor legislation. No one, I presume, would argue that we have not progressed in the recognition and protection of the rights of children.

He who would prefer the life of 1830 to the life of today must lack in charity for the weak and the unfortunate. Dorothea Dix, of Boston, was just beginning her efforts on behalf of the insane in the United States, efforts which in the middle of the century resulted in their being taken from the prison-kennels, the poor farms, or their own bewildered families and housed in special hospitals. Thomas H. Gallaudet, of Hartford, had shown the way by which the deaf and dumb might be set free, but the spread of this liberation remained for the times of his sons. Samuel Gridley Howe, of Boston, had not yet begun his pioneer enterprises for the blind and the feeble-minded.

In 1830 five-sixths of those incarcerated in the jails of New England and the Middle States were there upon complaints of creditors, the majority for debts of less than twenty dollars. It is true that thirteen years before New York had taken the lead in forbidding imprisonment for debts of less than twenty-five dollars, but in Philadelphia some were still confined for such debts as twenty-three cents or, in one case, two cents. For all New York's leniency there was at the end of the eighteen-twenties in Monroe County one imprisoned debtor for every ten families. It was 1832 before the state abolished the whole nefarious system. We say nothing here of human slavery on which the conscience of the country was just awakening; New England had acted in the previous generation, but New York in 1830 was only three years old as a free state. A considerable proportion of babies were born to die before the age of one year, but this was taken meekly as the way of God; mourning was a familiar badge of motherhood. That in the first quarter of the twentieth century infant mortality should be cut in half would have seemed to our great-great-grandmothers perhaps the greatest miracle of all. Summing up all these observations we are assured that the human spirit has been freed to an astonishing degree within the century just passed. We speak of the old time as a golden age of opportunity, but it was opportunity only for the physically strong.

We are scolded for our mechanization of industry as producing a material civilization inferior at bottom not only to the spiritual civilization of the Orient but to that obtaining here before the industrial revolution. We have forgotten how to contemplate, we are told; we have forgotten the uses of leisure. What such commentators have forgotten is that a century ago there was for most people little leisure to use. Let us look again at woman. If her place was in the home, let us view her there at daily work. A long day was necessary, oftentimes begun by candle light. Someone must make the candles. Someone must pump the water by hand and carry it to all the bedrooms. Someone must feed the wood into the big, voracious fireplaces on which alone depended the achievement of a tolerable temperature in winter time; someone must carry out the ashes; someone must be ready with the cloth to wipe away the dust that flew from the hearth about the room. The hearth presented other problems besides that of fuel supply. A generation accustomed to aluminum utensils would quake before the challenge of brass and copper pots and heavy iron pans and kettles, which had to be set on trivets or lifted up to sooty pothooks or notched trammels hanging from the crane or the less accessible crossbar bridging the chimney above the flames. Building a fire in the deep shaft-like oven at the side, then raking out the embers when it had heated well the surrounding bricks, then shoving in the bread loaves on the long board, all this was not as easy as telephoning to the bakery. It was not possible then for a young hostess resplendent in a dinner dress gaily to transfer from an electric range to a decorated table the concoctions she had poured not long since out of tin cans and paper packages. Commercial canning was not important until the days of the Civil War.

The transition of the box stove, especially that burning coal, which was just under way by 1830, was an important step in the emancipation of women, and not alone in lightening the drudgery of cooking. In the North it made it possible to heat rooms and not merely an area about the hearth, even to heat considerable portions of the house, a development to be completed a half-century later with the furnace; modern plumbing became practicable under a steady temperature and work was correspondingly reduced. The whole of clothing manufacture, with its carding apparatus, its spinning wheels, its looms, its cutting boards, has been transferred from the home.

Few phenomena at the beginning of the nineteenth century are more impressive to the modern reader than the immense effort required to "keep house" in those days. More women do more reading now than then, attend more concerts, meet each other in social contact, give more time to fewer children.

If the industrial revolution has drawn some women from kitchens into factories it has at the same time increased beyond all computation their opportunities for civilization. Only a little less can be said of its effect on man. A liberal Chinese philosopher has answered his compatriot critics of the West by reminding them that to use leisure one must have it. In the Far East it is the monopoly of the few; in the West it is coming to be the common lot.

It is scarcely to be hoped that all will use their leisure wisely; but at least we can survey the contrast in the opportunities for wise use. In 1830 the American public possessed no gallery of art; there were some good pictures in the few luxurious homes, but the proprietary miscellaneous museums in the cities gave a meagre shilling's worth to the visitor; there was little or no great music to be heard. There was no tax-supported public library in the country; today there are hundreds in this state alone. An historian of New England who is likewise a penetrating critic of modernity, Mr. J. T. Adams, is uncertain of the gain in art. He points out that our early settlers brought with them a habit of folk-art, that the farmer, whittling out utensils and the housewife working at her linen patterns, expressed themselves in terms of beauty and craftsmanship, and that a growing preoccupation with mere physical comfort, to say nothing of the concentration of industry in power-driven mills, has cut off this artistic function from the well-rounded individual. Supporting such a criticism, we might call to mind the singing schools of those old days when a contest between the singing societies of Stoughton and Dorchester aroused attention throughout the state. Perhaps the Handel and Haydn Society was as fine a thing in the Boston of 1830 as the symphony orchestra is in that of today. Perhaps the virtuoso has disheartened the amateur and the mass contents itself with being listeners and spectators, satisfied with receptivity. But I doubt it. An environment with lofty models will, according to all previous experience, stir general emulation. A simplicity enforced by poverty saved our ancestors from many grotesque blunders, for example, in the field of architecture, but in all times and places it has been wealth and sophistication which produced the soil of great art, and they seem likely to do so here as well.

Granted that New England transformed its seventeenth-century concern for salvation and its eighteenth-century concern for liberty into a nineteenth-century concern for social justice, there still remains the question as to whether or not it has grown in tolerance within the past one hundred years. In the first place it must be premised that a society that knows that it is right is seldom patient with dissent. "He that is willing to tolerate any religion," wrote the redoubtable Nathaniel Ward, of Ipswich, in 1647, "or discrepant way of religion besides his own, unless it be in matters merely indifferent, either doubts of his own or is not sincere in it." At the beginning of the nineteenth century some of the certainty had been lost in Massachusetts, discrepant ways were tolerated, though every man by state law still had to pay of his substance to support religion in some form. But complacency sat yet upon New England's brow. If, as William Stoughton had said five generations before, God had sifted a nation that he might send choice grain into the wilderness, the fruit was deemed most satisfactory. George Cabot in 1804 spoke loyally of "New England where there is among the body of the people more wisdom and virtue than in any other part of the United States." The section took no great interest in the rest of the country, and expected little interest from outsiders in itself. When, in 1820, Noah Webster was stirring up support for Amherst College, he solicited good will and possibly a contribution from Governor DeWitt Clinton. But at the end of the letter, as if discovering himself in an impropriety, he apologized for mentioning such a matter to a citizen of another state. The sentiment of moral self-sufficiency was not peculiar to New England; one found it in the South, the West, and in many smaller sections. As one fingers through the pages of Jedidiah Morse's geographies, one realizes how little the lad of that day could know about the folks of other places and other ways of life. Prejudice dissolves by contact. The railroad, the newspaper, and other agencies that bring men's minds together, all have made for understanding and for tolerance.

At the beginning of the nineteenth century, the largest city in this state had less than thirty thousand inhabitants and it had no near competitor. Some may deplore the trend that has brought the majority into towns. Serenity and the sturdy independence of the individual, they say, have been the price of it. There is no denying the force of such a criticism. How these habits of mind may be recovered must challenge the best thought of our sociologists. But contact and concentration are, in general, means to social progress. Progress, as a whole, is made by imitating what are judged to be better models. In towns the individual has before him men of many kinds; he is constantly though unconsciously selecting from them patterns such as he can copy. If his own old ways, in the light of his comparison, seem better, he has certainly lost nothing by the test itself; if he decides that other ways are better, then possibly he has gained. The development of town life since 1830 has inevitably enriched the culture of the country as a whole and been an element in progress, though our present-day society must take thought to save some of the virtues of the old-time isolation.

It is alleged by many that the growth of towns has brought a disproportionate growth of crime, that it worked faster toward degeneration than toward progress. It is true that it is apparently breaking down the family discipline so coercive a hundred years ago; it is true that with the accumulation of surplus there are more numerous and ingenious crimes against property than when there was little to steal. The modern means of motion facilitate escape so as to make crime safer and therefore more attractive and more frequent. But this does not mean that the criminal impulse is more generally distributed now than then. Crime was fairly safe along the Natchez Trail at the beginning of the nineteenth century and it was frequent. The bankers on the Carolina coast and the smugglers of Amelia Island prospered mightily. But here in New England there were public executions often enough to keep the people entertained with holidays. If any doubt that rogues could flourish in the pure air of that time and this very region he may be referred to three old books, all of which have been reprinted within the present decade: *The Memoirs of the Notorious Stephen Burroughs*, *The Life and Adventures of Henry Tufts*, and *The Life of Captain Lightfoot*. The Reverend Richard S. Storrs in his Fiftieth Anniversary Sermon looked back on the days when he became the pastor of Braintree in 1810. There was then, he thought, far more "brawling, shameless intoxication, quarreling, profaneness, vulgarity, and licentiousness; . . . wine and spirits were imbibed at funerals to quiet the nerves and move the lachrymals of attendants [and] rowdyism and fisticuffs triumphed over law and order in town-meetings, muster and election days." Apparently in some towns, at least, there was more evil-doing in the good old times than now, just as there were proportionately more poor to care for. In Ecclesiastes (VII,10) there is a verse which bears upon this point: "Say not thou, what is the cause that former days were better than these, for thou dost not inquire wisely concerning this." It is difficult to say whether or not the individual American of 1930 is better than his ancestor of 1830, that is to say, more brave, more generous, more true, but in many ways the social mind has become more sympathetic and more just.

THOREAU AND THE MACHINE AGE

THOREAU AND THE MACHINE AGE

BY HENRY SEIDEL CANBY

A SMALLISH man but long-legged, firm set, with high cheek bones like an Indian's, a powerful nose, and gray-blue eyes—"terrible eyes," as Emerson said, that looked you through and through, his face bearded in later life, but in mid-career islanded in soft brown whiskers, dressed always for rough walking, an old music book under one arm for pressing flowers, an umbrella often as not in the other hand—even in the Maine woods he carried an umbrella. Here was Thoreau, as by luck you might have seen him in the brush or swamps, or crossing the Concord road by a fox path. And this is the man, whose essay "Civil Disobedience," coming into the hands of a Hindu barrister in South Africa in 1907, left ideas and title so firmly implanted that when a score of years later that student had become the greatest moral force in India and was known wherever news goes as Mahatma Gandhi, it was the name of Thoreau's essay which he used in English for his political policy. Gandhi's passive, self-sufficing civil disobedience has roots in Concord. Little wonder that, even in that town of peripatetic philosophers, Thoreau was a marked and markable man.

With reason, for here was one of the world's rare originals whose eccentricity comes from being too sane. The farms of Concord, he said, were his by right of free enjoyment: he had the best of them, the air, the soil, the flowers, the views; he got their best crops. In like fashion, Thoreau got the best of Concord itself, was its eye and central mind when the others, even sometimes Emerson, were limbs merely that went sprawling about business of no ultimate concern. He was the man most alive in Concord. Few men of his day are more alive than he in the modern world.

His life is well known in its relation to nature. We have had him for years as the patron of walking clubs and bird study societies, and the excerpts in which he is usually read are taken almost exclusively from his nature descriptions. He was a lover of nature who tried over-conscientiously to turn his love into science and often spoiled good writing by wearisome detail and good science by inaccuracy and absent-mindedness. Nevertheless, and certainly at his best, he unites seer and lover in his nature studies in happy union. He was always positive there with that tranquillity of mind that knows no rebellion. Had he been as concerned with turning his life as a nature man into art as with directing that life towards some end approved by the New England conscience he would very simply and easily have taken his place in the literary hierarchy beside

Izaak Walton, Hudson, Herrick, Marvell, Sidney.

But there are negative Thoreaus also: a protestant Thoreau, radical, rebel, economist, puritan—an unwilling Thoreau who turned aside from his proper business with nature to protest against a society which bent a man towards its own misdirected aims; and again, a puzzled Thoreau, whose conscience would not let him escape a duty to the minds of his fellow-men although he so readily shrugged off their companionship. Conscience also, he said, has its diseases.

The positive Thoreau is all rugged tenderness and shrewd and happy contemplation. He is not a mystic, and yet would have lived happily with his philosophy, fishing with Walton in "a wide halo of ease and leisure." But the negative Thoreau is either a seeker, eager to justify his idea of truth, or a fighter against a society that will not let him alone. It is this latter phase that I wish to discuss, where the whimsical, the religious Thoreau of the "Week on the Concord and Merrimac Rivers" becomes spark and flint. Both the negative Thoreaus are puritan. It was his innate puritanism as much as the austerity of his Concord environment which made him try to moralize nature. The two million words of his Journal are a tribute to duty. It was no essential part of his scheme of independent and individual living, that he should set it all down, try to rationalize it for others. The positive Thoreau

7

would have been content with poetry and essays, the puritan Thoreau must prepare a vast storehouse of ammunition by which the world might eventually be driven towards truth. It was the puritan Thoreau that turned, like an angry woodchuck on an interfering world, lashed it with invective, scorned its idleness, prepared at Walden a thoughtful answer to the argument of industrialism that you must produce or be barbarous. I am concerned here with Emerson's "protestant à l'outrance," whose influence extends today from the Merrimac to the Ganges. I am concerned still more with the individualist who, when Deacon Brown offered a pledge at the peace meeting, that they should treat all mankind as brothers henceforth, remarked, "I think I shall wait and see how they treat me first."

It is not nature that he defends in his writings, but himself. If his zest had been for textual criticism, or contemplating his navel, his cause would have been the same, his indignation equal, his argument as sound. Of the two Thoreaus, the one belongs to Concord, and, as I hope to show, with the true discoverers of America. The other is an individualist citizen of the universe, who will not endure interference with his idea of living. He is a belated perfectionist set in sudden opposition to the new industrial slant of Western civilization, a Milton attacking, not despots, but machines. This Thoreau belongs definitely and without reference to aesthetic values in the world movements of our time, and has a place in intellectual history which only the ignorant will belittle because his stance was merely Walden Pond and the village life of Concord.

I shall not trace his protest against our civilization through his books and his Journal, but rather try to sum it up from his total conclusions. It is implicit in the "Week," which is a youthful book, lacking a theme and over-stuffed with quotation, a record of a young man's thoughts when his reading inter-mingled with fresh experience. In that first sturdy chapter in "Walden," called "Economy," it comes out clear in a terse and powerful prose. "Civil Disobedience" and "Life Without Principle" are rebellion simon-pure.

For Thoreau's morality was that a soul should be

> Born to its own affairs,
> Its own joys and own cares.

His affairs were "his Master's business, and his own joy." They seemed to him transcendentally im-portant, and to them he devoted his leisure. He was able to support himself in a number of ways, by pencil-making, surveying, teaching, more doubtfully by lecturing, but no one of them could produce what Concord called a livelihood, without impinging on his priceless leisure. His happiness was to observe and meditate, and that was his duty also. If he could not think, he was, as he complains so often, asleep—no longer alive in the Elizabethan sense, no longer useful to himself, or even to Concord, for Massachusetts will get on well enough without his pencils, but may take profit from his wisdom drawn from swamps and woods.

But in an America made by hard work on the land and now growing rich strenuously by steam and water, rails and looms, sauntering is peculiarly misunderstood, nature unprofitable except when dead, science idle unless in terms of measurement, religion suspect out of church. Thoreau is in a society unfit for the honest leisure that leads to mental enrichment, and that makes him mad. Madder still, because the pressure of subsistence upon opportunity is not heavy in New England. Food and shelter are readily had. It is easy to live, if hard to grow rich.

Thoreau's predecessors on American soil had found their leisure on the frontier. The wastrels and the idlers, the adventurers and the ne'er-do-wells, had taken to the woods, lived crudely in its plenty, drifted the streams, hunted in the forests, been so content, many of them, that it was a real question in the early 1800's whether the white man in the West would not accept the *mores* of the Indian. Thoreau envied the Indian, but not the pioneer white. He would have been content, I think, to accept savagery, but not barbarism. He had a mind to satisfy, and cultivated desires that asked more than a franchise in the wilderness. He needed books, companionship with his peers, leisure to study as well as to observe, to observe as well as to get food. His problem was a problem for civilization. Ten wild Americas could never solve it, and it is noteworthy that this lover of wilderness seldom speaks of the West, still untamed in his day, and made no strong attempts to see it until near the end of his life. He had nature in Concord; when he went to the Maine woods, it was to learn how the Indian lived.

His problem was normal, not abnormal; it was the dilemma which confronts millions of men and women in our phase of the industrial revolution. Culture and education have given them tastes and intellectual cravings which only leisure can satisfy; and our habit of life has crammed them with material wants, for clothes, machines, cleanliness, amusement, and all the refinements of a highly mechanical environment. But leisure and luxury, or even leisure and comfort, they cannot have together. They must produce if they are to enjoy production, they must produce if the industrial machine is to keep functioning. Up and up goes the standard of living, lifted like the steel shafts of a skyscraper by all the engines of advertising. There is no end to wanting, because new necessities are created in endless succession. The best part of a life is spent in "earning money in order to enjoy a questionable liberty during the least valuable part of it." Energy is dissipated in seeking "anxiously to be developed, to subject yourself to many influences to be played on." Bound to the wheel of the world, blind, and drunk with its speed, caught in the economics of production where want breeds want, we are citizens of a mad world where ends are lost in means of living. Concord or New York—there is little difference between Farmer Brown expanding his acres until he dies crushed by them, or the corporation lawyer working twelve hours a day in pursuit of a phantom competence which is never enough. There is only this difference as Thoreau already saw in Concord: a mounting curve, which industrialism was to push towards its logical conclusion. His dilemma is the true subsistence problem of the industrial revolution, which gave us control of nature without control of ourselves. The mediaeval donkey with his bundle of hay has become a modern mechanical ass with automobiles, airplanes, the Riviera, Park Avenue, and bootleg champagne hung before his straining eyes. We can never catch up—and leisure lies beyond.

The problem, of course, in its essence is ancient, and it is because Thoreau found it so succinctly stated in Hindu and Chinese philosophy that he is so Oriental in his quoting. Gandhi found in "Civil Disobedience" ideas from his own India restated in new terms forced by new conditions created in the

West. But Thoreau was no Oriental. Like Emerson, he was a Westerner, a Yankee, who wanted to do, not to be. Contemplating the navel is not his desideratum. He wants leisure, yes, but leisure to be happy in his own individualistic fashion, and to make use of his happiness. He went to Walden Pond "because I wish to live deliberately, to front only the essential facts of life, and see if I could not learn what it had to teach, and not, when I came to die, discover that I had not lived. I did not wish to live what was not life, living is so dear; nor did I wish to practise resignation, unless it was quite necessary. I wanted to live deep and suck out all the marrow of life, to live . . . sturdily and Spartan-like, . . . to drive life into a corner and reduce it to its lowest terms, and, if it proved to be mean, why then to get the whole and genuine meanness of it, and publish its meanness to the world; or if it were sublime, to know it by experience. . . . Our life is frittered away in detail. . . . I say, let your affairs be as two or three, and not a hundred or a thousand; instead of a million count half a dozen, and keep your accounts on your thumb nail. In the midst of this chopping sea of civilized life, . . . a man has to live . . . by dead reckoning. . . . Simplify, simplify. . . . The nation . . . is cluttered with furniture and tripped up by its own traps, ruined by luxury and needless expense, by want of calculation and a worthy aim. . . . It lives too fast. . . . We

do not ride on the railroad; it rides upon us. . . .
As for work, we haven't any of consequence. We
have the Saint Vitus dance, and cannot possibly
keep our heads still. . . . Hardly a man takes a
half hour's nap after dinner, but when he wakes
he holds up his head and asks, 'What's the news?'
. . . When we are unhurried and wise, we perceive
that only great and worthy things have any perma-
nent and absolute existence. . . . Children, who play
life, discern its true law and relations more clearly
than men, who fail to live it worthily, but who
think that they are wiser by experience, that is, by
failure. . . . Let us spend one day as deliberately
as Nature, and not be thrown off the track by every
nutshell and mosquito's wing that falls on the rails.
. . . If you stand right fronting and face to face to
a fact, you will see the sun glimmer on both its
surfaces, as if it were a cimiter, and feel its sweet edge
dividing you through the heart and marrow, and
so you will happily conclude your mortal career."
"If we respected only what is inevitable and has a
right to be, music and poetry would resound along
the streets."

Thoreau went to Walden Pond to make a book
from his Journal, to live under such circumstances as
would permit him, the individualist, seer, and
nature lover, to be useful and happy in a high sense,
but most of all to prove that in an acquisitive society,
based upon production and proceeding by competi-

tion, a man could do what he most wanted, even if there were no cash profits in it, and still subsist.

Stevenson's idea that Thoreau was dodging life and its responsibilities is nonsense from a romanticist whose sacrifices were all capitalized. When Thoreau went to Walden, he walked towards the problem, not away from it. His answer was not an Oriental renunciation of all worldly things, whose logical conclusion is a seat in the dust and scraps of food from the faithful. His answer was renunciation of whatever does not primarily concern *you*—a sifting and threshing of desire until the chaff of imposed wants flies upward and the good grain of essential need remains. For Henry Thoreau, the woods, books, enough solitude, and the simplest food and clothing were prerequisites for successful leisure. "Walden" records the results of the experiment, and note that an equal emphasis in that well-digested book falls upon the fruits of happy contemplation and the means by which it was secured. The actual cash account of Thoreau's living is there, carefully set down. It is not your living, your wants—but he asked neither you nor anyone to come to Walden, and if he implores the generality to bind themselves like Ulysses to the mast of higher pleasure until the wasteful meridian of the dinner hour is past, that is his little joke upon hungry Transcendentalists who had to eat at a table. His is a type solution of which the principle is applicable in a thousand fashions.

When he had enough of solitude (one factor only in his need) and another way of beating foolish labor around the bush offered itself, he left Walden and came to live with Emerson. Walden had served its purpose.

If the early converts to the British Labor Party carried copies of "Walden" in their pockets, and knew long passages by heart, it was not because they hoped to set up housekeeping in the New Forest or upon Wordsworth's lakes. They saw that the idea of the book was not life in nature, but life for the sake of living, and how to live it. Living for them was a different problem from life in Thoreau's semi-rustic world, but the principle was the same. Let us reform our ends and reconstruct our means so that each human shall be able to live in his own best way. It can be done—if not by going to Walden Pond, then by shortening hours of labor, distributing the products of machinery, and educating desire until we get and enjoy only the best.

Thoreau challenges the industrial order because he asks the fundamental question, where are you going, what do you really want? It was not a question in abstract philosophy merely. A German, named J. A. Etzler, published first in Pennsylvania, and then later in England, a book called "The Paradise Within Reach of all Men, Without Labor, by Powers of Nature and Machinery." Thoreau reviewed the second English edition of 1842 in *The*

Democratic Review in 1843. It was a book that with much romantic and sometimes absurd speculation, outlined the possible results, for comfort and power, of the use of machinery. The prophetic German prepared a control of nature by machinery and called upon mankind to create an immediate Utopia. There is not one of his descriptions of machine power quoted by Thoreau in his review that has not by now been fully realized. All the man lacked was specific knowledge of processes, all that is wrong in the scheme is the time element (ten years instead of a century), and his guess at the result for the human race. We are not so happy nor so comfortable as he thought.

Thoreau is neither incredulous of the Etzlerian dream, nor dazzled by its possibilities. He strikes at the root of the fallacy: "The chief fault of this book is that it aims to secure the greatest degree of gross comfort and pleasure merely. Nature is to be controlled, wealth is to be controlled, pleasure is to be distributed by a corporation, and not the slightest concern for the moral control of man and his wants." The horsepower of machinery is trusted for everything, and nothing said of the horsepower of love. Faith in that is the first reform; with that we could do without machinery. In physics, we can make the elements work for us, but to what use unless the moral force is also brought under control. "Nothing can be effected but by one man," the converse of which is that unless the man himself is clarified, machinery can add only to gross comfort and irking wants.

Thoreau's review is playful, but his life experiment in controlled living was as earnest as it was happy. His challenge to the industrial order came from a central principle of his nature thoroughly rationalized. He was obstinate, but clear-eyed. There is really no other solution than his to the increasing ills of a state which we call sometimes progressive, but more often strenuous, nervous, febrile, aimless. The disease—which like some selective malady, seizes upon our best, and fills sanitariums with nervous wrecks, homes with neurotics, cities with fine-drawn, irritable men, slaves of time whose hopes of leisure, and with leisure happiness, are always deferred—is susceptible to no other cure. Psychiatrists are patchers and repairers merely. They and the vocabulary of their science are inventions to describe the malady which Thoreau diagnosed. They cannot save the machine, and freely admit it. The only cure is moral, the only alleviation a robust discrimination in wants. Curious that our continent should provide the readiest escape into nature, where leisure is easiest, and the most damning industrial competition! Curious, but inevitable. We have had the most nature to control, and diverted from the ends of common sense the most energy in order to control for the sake of production. Babbitt was a symbol and a symptom of power turning into weakness. If Sinclair Lewis created him out of a thousand prototypes, Thoreau philosophized him in advance of his nativity. If nervous indigestion is the American disease, Thoreau is surely the American Philosopher. And he might have excepted his Journal when he wrote, in "Life without Principle," that there is "little or nothing to be remembered written on the subject of . . . how to make getting a living not merely honest and honorable, but altogether inviting and glorious."

It was Thoreau the protestant, again, who wrote the essay on "Civil Disobedience." This time it was the state, not an economic system, which interfered with his individualism. When the state lets him alone, he will ignore the state, but if it forces him to participate in injustice then he is as wronged as when society refuses him leisure. I do not take his remarks upon slavery, which the Mexican question in 1849 had made an issue of violence, too seriously. Slavery was repugnant to every fibre of a professional wanderer, and it was easy to be an Abolitionist in Concord. He was far sounder in his clear view that Massachussets practises wage slavery than in his willingness to see the Southern knot cut by a single gesture. But his defense of his own integrity is unimpeachable. The state exists for individuals, not individuals for the state; patriotism is less then private morality; if the minority yields to the majority in essential matters it is soiled by the compromise. Only an honest man can be a good citizen. To force the support of injustice, even by so indirect a method as taxation, is an offense against moral liberty. When men resist on conscience they are irresistible. That is Gandhi's idea also. Thoreau went to jail gladly on the issue, and indifferently came out. It seemed to him a petty experience—for the state. But with a community of Thoreaus to deal with, the experience is not petty.

"Civil Disobedience" and "Life without Principle" are the most radical essays in American literature, precisely because they do not threaten property, or counsel spoiling the fat for the benefit of the lean, but go to the root of the whole matter, where it is made clear that a life conducted for worthy ends and according to principles of elementary justice is the ultimate which must be preserved even if the state totters. Like Falstaff, they offend only the virtuous who have their own principles to lose. Admit this, make the individual responsible, and government becomes a machine, best liked when least noted. Politics and the routine of administration are "*infra*-human, a kind of vegetation," to be thought of as little as possible, *unless* they interfere; then there is only one answer to the state and that is to oppose it.

Such theories are dangerous, for they challenge the success of a state as such, if it is not the success of men, and deny it the moral standards of expediency by which every state lives. When the Thoreaus and Gandhis rebel, there is no compromise. They cannot, like our own radicals, be satisfied by stopping their mouths with prosperity. But it is questionable whether Thoreau would have thought it worth his while actively to conspire and rebel. He did not want to reform society, he wanted to reform himself. Even the execution of John Brown could not rouse him that far. He would have given his life for his own principles, but would have been sparing of his energies in the doubtful endeavor to remake an institution for the benefit of other men. He was first of all an individualist. Let each man save himself and all will be saved. You cannot quash such a theory by saying that it leads to anarchy.

The most outspoken doctrines of resistance ever penned on this continent have been seldom mentioned in radical literature. They are too utterly un-European, too much the exact antithesis of either socialism or communism, which are industrialism's particular parasites; and that is perhaps why they have found their first broad application in the East. They require the kind of courage that only individuals possess, and while we have had radical parties enough, we have not had enough Thoreaus to overturn a state. And yet there is more dynamite in his writing for Americans than in all Marxism. We might conceivably, even yet, become radical his way.

The battle between the city and the country reaches one of its climaxes in Thoreau. The conflict between two ways of life, which is a deeper and longer conflict than any merely economic struggle, was sharply visible from Walden. He did not make the mistake of thinking that a man was a country-man because he lived in the country, nor commit the fallacy of praising labor with the plough in contrast to labor at the machine. He was free from this kind of sentimentalism, spared perhaps because the horrid results of factory life were less visible in New than in Old England. He was concerned rather with the deeper difference between accord with nature and its exploitation. The costliness of crowd living, the creation of artificial wants, the loss of aim in a hurried and fretful life, and an obsession with the means of living—these are what he meant by city life. He spoke of other disabilities—gaiety, license, convention, the dissipation of time valuable for a naturalist and a philosopher. But these are the whims of a puritan solitary. On the art of social living his views are about as valuable as his criticism of music and architecture. He knew Maine better than Boston, and because he was a right judge of sunsets cannot be allowed to deprecate a taste in wine. One may admire him and still tolerate Voltaire, Alcibiades, Pope, and Anatole France, even though none could have been happy overnight at Walden.

THOREAU AND THE MACHINE AGE

The democratic man who, seizing his spiritual opportunities, should rise to all that Whitman and Thoreau offered, has, of course, never bestirred himself. He has taken, rather, to city life with rapture, and has filled the environs of every great city, and Walden itself, with blazing symbols of every abomination in Thoreau's calendar. The excrements of the city lie on the countryside. We have all risen like hungry fish to the lure of new desires. We want more a hundred times than in 1840, and advertising sets new wants before us in triplicate. We have sold our individualism to the radio, the newspaper, the weekly illustrated magazine, and the moving picture. We have accepted the ideology of a business world which believes that man at hard labor is the noblest work of God. A Thoreauvian must think that there is more energy than health in American civilization, more noise than aim, more childish intent to pile block on block than philosophic consideration for the happiness of man. Yet like children we have learned something in our play. We have gone through that necessary stage where the means for living without digressive effort are readily provided. Machinery, not the Transcendentalists, made this possible. The plain man has acquired civilized luxuries, if not civilized tastes. He has learned how to be comfortable, if not how to be happy. He has leisure if he wants it, and lacks only either the knowledge or the will to control his own future according to ends that may be regarded as best. In this last, men by no means plain are no better off. We are ripe for a dose of Thoreau.

But it takes, at least in the industrialized West, an aristocrat to read him. In spite of his rough boots, worn coat, and brusque manners he was every ounce an aristocrat himself. He had his idea of what a man owed to himself. He had his code. It is clear that wealth and material power and, what is more unfortunate, dynamic ideas, are in the hands today of men whose keenness does not compensate for their lack of insight and of self-knowledge. One kind of aristocracy died with the old South in the Civil War, and if it had survived might have taught us something of value in social intercourse now almost lost. Another aristocracy waned with the New England individualists, and this was the more valuable because its discriminate renunciation and its positive grip upon fine thinking are not only in sharper opposition to the tendencies of mass living, but far more transferable to the conditions of that life. We can provide Waldens anywhere today if we can breed the men to want them. We must breed Thoreaus somewhere, or see this machine society stuffed and stifled by its own super-heated desires. One cannot walk down Broadway without praising God that sane men once did live here. Thoreau is their prophet.

THOREAU AND THE MACHINE AGE

He is not dead yet. He is more alive than Emerson, because he wrote better, because the oversoul at best can stir us on to metaphysics, whereas a possible way of happy living is a need at every man's door. There is still a minority determined to live their own best lives, which is what one has to do in order to become a Thoreauvian.

Editorial Note. This essay appeared in the March number of *The Yale Review* of 1931, and is also a part of a chapter on Thoreau in Mr. Canby's *Classic Americans,* which is to appear in the autumn of 1931.

INDEX